the psalms in other words

the psalms in other words

A PRESENTATION FOR BEGINNERS

by

Dom Hubert van Zeller

TEMPLEGATE

SPRINGFIELD, ILLINOIS

248
Val

Nihil obstat: RALPH RUSSELL, *Censor Deputatus*
Imprimatur: B. C. BUTLER, *Abb. Pres.*
26. vi. 63

For Deen and Dorth,
to take the place of the one that
was thrown out

Preface

THE FIRST THING to be understood is that this is *not* a translation of the psalter. Anyone who takes the trouble to compare what follows with the psalms as they are printed in the Bible will see at once that the 'in other words' of the title of this book could read 'in *quite* other words.' I am aiming at only an abstract or digest. I have looked at each psalm as it comes along for its particular theme, and the purpose has been to convey this theme in a language intelligible, reverent, more or less contemporary and more or less poetic. With such a loose framework proposed, it has seemed legitimate to leave out not only verses and whole groups of verses but also some of the repetitions, historical allusions, vindictive passages and controversial expressions with which the psalter abounds. So what this book tries to do is to give the feel of the psalter to people who might otherwise be put off by its length, language, and obscurity. The hope is that from the prayerful use of this rendering the reader will go directly to the inspired words. Wherever the actual text of the psalms is quoted in these pages it appears in italics, and such verses are of course the ones on which to concentrate. Certainly there is no attempt in the versions here submitted either to go one better than the Holy Spirit, or to present an alternative psalter, or to provide a commentary. The sole attempt is to turn the reader's attention to the earliest of the prayer-books of the faithful and to inspire him with the desire to make the psalmist's prayer his own.

Psalm 1

To walk with sinners is sadness. It is the soul who is searching for God's will, and who is always trying to do it, who is happy.

The man who does not waste his time with the wicked, but ponders instead upon his duty towards God, is rooted deep. He is like a tree well watered: he yields fruit and his leaves stay green.

Such security is not for the wicked. The wicked are never at rest: they are rootless, forever tossed about. So when it comes to the judgment of the just and the sinful, the wicked shall not be there to take the place prepared for each soul in heaven.

For the Lord watches over the way of the just, but the way of the wicked vanishes. Where there are no foundations, there is nothing for God's grace to act upon.

✠

Psalm 2

Why does the world resist the Lord? How foolish for mere man to pit his strength against God's. How idle to plan the destruction of those whom the Lord has called his own. God only laughs at such presumption.

'You think to overthrow the ruler whom I have enthroned' says God, 'but when the ruler is son of mine, then there is no dethroning him. Let this son of mine ask what he will, and I am at his side to grant it.'

So take warning, you worldly rulers, for those who resist this son of his shall be broken like so many brittle platters. Your safety lies in surrendering to the Lord. Serve him then in fear of punishment, and in joyous knowledge of his mercies. *Happy are all who take refuge in him.*

9

Psalm 3

Many there are who work against me. They say I shall get no help from God.

My reply is that God hears my prayers. Awake or asleep, I am all the time supported by him. He is my safety.

So I am not alarmed by the numbers of those who attack me. I know I shall be heard when I cry out, as I do now, for help.

For you strike my enemies on the cheek; the teeth of the wicked you break. Salvation is the Lord's and upon your people be your blessing.

☦

Psalm 4

Lord, answer me when I call upon you. Have pity and hear my prayer. You are my relief in the time of trouble.

I keep telling the leaders, the men of influence, how foolish they are to strive after what is unreal and untrue. How much longer will they keep their hearts closed against grace? If only they knew what wonders you do for the soul who is faithful.

Let these men of the world dwell upon the thought of God in silence, in compunction, and in trust. So many of them look forward to better things in this life, but the Lord himself is better than any of his gifts.

It is you, Lord, who puts happiness into my heart. It is not the things of this world that make me happy. From you alone comes the peace which I enjoy. I do not lie awake at night; I know that you are my security. You are the source and ground of my hope.

☦

Psalm 5

Listen to my prayers, Lord, to my sorrowful cry for help. You are my king and my God. To you I raise my voice in the morning.

Not for the malicious are your graces; not for the proud, the cruel, the insincere, the disloyal, the untruthful.

But I, because of your abundant kindness, will enter your house. I will worship at your holy temple in fear of you, O Lord.

Only show me the way you want me to take. The way of those who are not serious, the way of the frivoluous and superficial, leads nowhere.

Those who make you their refuge are secure in their trust. Bless, O Lord, those who serve you thus.

☦

Psalm 6

My body and soul suffer anguish: I dread the consequences of my sins. There is fear in my heart, for I know how justly I deserve your punishments.

Come to my rescue, Lord, and in your mercy heal me. If I once despair I shall be as a dead man. And neither praise nor gratitude goes up to you from a corpse.

I am constantly bewailing my wretchedness (every night I cry about it in bed), and the only hope I have left is your readiness to forgive.

So long as I know that you have heard my call for help, I am confident that my trials will be overcome.

☦

Psalm 7

In you, Lord God, I take my refuge. All around me are those who wish me evil. Let me not fall into their hands.

If there is reason for their malice, then willingly I submit to punishment. But whatever evil I have done is known by you to have been of folly and not of set purpose.

11

I trust in your mercy and I believe in my own good faith. It is those who are in bad faith who offend you. No friend of mine has received from me deliberate hurt.

Oh yes, Lord, you are right to punish us when we sin deliberately—I would be the first to admit my guilt—but there is always room in my soul for praise and gratitude. I give praise to your justice and gratitude for your mercy.

May the sinful acknowledge their sins and be converted. All they do in their sins is to dig pits which they must fall into later on. By sinning they only heap up misery for themselves.

☩

Psalm 8

O Lord, how glorious is your name over all the earth. Nature gives praise to you and so does man. Even the smallest infant, though unconsciously, praises your name.

What are we humans that we should receive such graces from your hands? And as for the Messias, man and God in one, *you have given him rule over the works of your hands, putting all things under his feet.*

The whole of creation is his possession. Sheep, oxen, birds, fishes: all are his. No wonder your name is glorious over every part of the earth.

☩

Psalm 9

With all my heart I thank you, Lord, for turning back the forces drawn up against me. My gladness is your gift to me, and I in return give praise to your name.

Your power has triumphed over the power of man, and I rejoice that you will rule for ever and ever.

In times of trouble you give us strength, and so long as we trust in you we know that we shall not be forsaken.

12

But my trials are not over yet, and though I have been rescued by you from the worst evils I call upon you for further graces.

Remember, Lord, that the needy shall not go uncomforted, *nor shall the hope of the afflicted forever perish.*

Why, Lord, do you stand so far off? There are times when you seem unconcerned about our distress. Why such indifference to our cause?

Often the wicked have it all their own way. 'There is no God' they say, 'we can manage our affairs without God's help.' And, sure enough, it looks for a time as though they are settled and secure.

They commit every sort of sin, and tell themselves that God has forgotten about them, has not seen what they have done, has given up interest.

Why should the wicked man despise God, saying in his heart, 'He will not avenge it?' You do see; you are concerned; you have not forgotten.

Rise, O Lord . . . lift up your hand . . . forget not the afflicted. You see our human misery and sorrow just as you see our evil thoughts and acts. Misery and sorrow are for your handling, are for your healing. It is to you that the wretched look for help.

☫

Psalm 10

My refuge is in God. To those who advise me to flee like a bird to the mountains I answer that, if the Lord allows it, an arrow can bring down a bird as well in the mountains as in the plain.

It is rather to the temple that I would flee, or to the very throne of God in heaven. Where God is, there lies my safety.

The eyes of God look down and see the poor man's plight. They search the just man's case and the sinner's. Where they see violence, the eyes of God show anger.

For the Lord is just; he loves just deeds. The upright shall see his face.

13

Psalm 11

Help me, Lord, for holiness is rare, and there is none to stand by me. Loyalty, trust, truth: these things have vanished from among us.

Everyone lies. People say smooth things to one another, but their hearts are divided.

May the Lord pluck out these false and double tongues. There are those who say, 'Our lips are our own . . . who is to tell us what to speak?'

May the Lord grant safety to those who long for it. May he rise up and fulfil his promises. *The promises of the Lord are sure.* There is no doubt but that the Lord will save us.

All around us are sinners walking with their heads high. The basest of men fill the topmost positions. *But you will keep us and preserve us always from this generation.*

Psalm 12

You are forgetting me, O Lord. For how long will this go on? *How long will you hide your face from me?*

Sorrow is lodged in my soul. Day after day it is the same. Must it be always like this? *Look, answer me, O Lord my God.*

Give me the grace not to die in this state or the forces of evil will boast of having won. It would be bad if my enemies could point to my downfall—especially since they know that I trusted in you.

Let my heart be glad in grace. I want to be able to praise you, and to say at the end, 'God has been good to me.'

Psalm 13

A man is a fool if he says, 'There is no God.' But many are foolish enough to say this, and bad enough to act upon it.

Hardly anyone does good any more, or seeks God. God looks down from heaven upon mankind to see if there is even one soul who seriously searches for him in truth.

Does he see so much as one? All go after their own desires; they are not interested in serving God. Certainly they never call upon his name.

It will go hard with such souls when God comes out finally on the side of the just. God has pledged himself to be the refuge of his servants—however laboriously such servants may wilt under pressure.

O, that out of Sion would come the salvation of Israel. When the Lord restores the well-being of his people, then shall Jacob exult and Israel be glad.

☦

Psalm 14

Lord, tell me whom you have invited to be your guests. What qualities do you expect of those who are to occupy your tent, who are to live on your holy mountain?

But I know the answer already. It must be those who act uprightly, justly, sincerely, and who speak no evil of others. It must be those who refuse to inflict injury, who shun the ways of the wicked, who want rather to be among those who fear God.

It must be those also who keep their promises in spite of what loss they may suffer by doing so. It must be those who do not go in for usury or for bribery. *He who does these things shall never be disturbed.*

☦

Psalm 15

Look after me, Lord, for I have put all my hope in you. I tell you truly, 'You are my all. Apart from you I have no good.'

It is because of this that you have made me value the company of holy people. I have something in common with those who serve you. As for those who serve other gods, they are no friends of mine.

You have given yourself to be my whole life, and I must cling to that. What could be more beautiful than to live in such a setting?

I give praise to you for letting me see things in this way. I know that so long as I hold to this view of life I shall not be unsettled. Outwardly and inwardly I am established in confidence —in you.

You are not one to let a devoted servant go under. *You will show me the path to life, fullness of joys in your presence, the delights at your right hand for ever.*

✠

Psalm 16

Listen to my appeal, Lord, for this heartfelt cry is justified. Knowing that you judge fairly, I leave the outcome of my request to you.

Try me in any way you will, you cannot find it in me to rebel. I have set myself to obey your law, and I pray that you may keep me to this course.

I have called out to you because in the past you have heard me. Hear me again now, O my God. Repeat once more your mercies—as you do towards those who place their hope in you.

Shelter me under your wing; there are some who are violently opposed to me. By your hand, by your sword, deliver me.

Mortal men may rage against me, but I have confidence in appearing without reproach before your face. *I shall be content in your presence.*

✠

Psalm 17

I love you, O Lord, my strength. You are *my rock, my fortress, my deliverer.* 'Praised be the Lord,' I exclaim, 'and I am safe from my enemies.'

Though tossed about by the waves of death, though overwhelmed by floods of destruction, I cried out to God. And from his temple he heard me.

He inclined the heavens and came down to me. He reached out from on high and grasped me. He drew me out of the deep waters. It is because he loves me that he has done this.

For my part I have done my best, keeping to his ways and obeying his commandments. And the Lord has rewarded me accordingly.

Toward the faithful you are faithful, toward the wholehearted you are wholehearted, toward the sincere you are sincere. You bring salvation to the humble, to the proud you bring humiliation.

My lamp is alight only because of you. The darkness which is all about me becomes light while you are here.

With you at my side I can face an armed force; with you to show me I can scale a wall.

Your promises hold good. You are a shield to all who come to you for shelter. Whatever I know of human skills, of the craft of war, has come to me through your grace. Your right hand has held me up, you have guided my steps. If I have been successful in battle it is because you have given me the victory.

Therefore I will proclaim you, O Lord, among the nations, and I will sing praise to your name, you who gave great victories to your king and showed kindness to your anointed, to David and his posterity forever.

☦

Psalm 18

The heavens proclaim the glory of God; the sky is a declaration of God's workmanship. The whole of creation, from the firmament to the succession of days, is witness to God's grandeur. It is a message, too, which we need to read aright.

Why else, if not to impart knowledge, has God pitched a tent up there for the sun? Heat following cold, light following darkness: these things are for our instruction.

The law of the Lord is perfect, refreshing the soul. Whether it is the law of nature or the law of right conduct, the law of the Lord brings wisdom to the simple of heart. All that the Lord commands is right, enlightening, clear, and brings happiness to those to accept it.

The law of the Lord is even sweet, sweeter than honey, to those who want to be nourished by it.

Lord, you know my intention to be faithful. But there· must be failings, failings which I do not clearly see, in my fidelity. Cleanse me, O Lord, of these unacknowledged faults. I mean to be blameless before you—innocent anyway of serious sin.

May this intention, expressed here deliberately in word, be pleasing to you, O God my support and my deliverer.

☩

Psalm 19

May God hear you in the day of your sorrow; may his power protect you. May help reach you from his sanctuary, from Sion.

May he remember all your offerings, accepting the sacrifices you have made to him. May he grant your heart's desire, confirming your every plan.

May we be able to rejoice in your success, bearing witness in public to the glory of God's name. May he listen to all your prayers.

Now I know that the Lord has given victory to his anointed, that he has answered him from his holy heaven.

Some place their trust in chariots, some in horses. For us to place our trust in the name of the Lord. Where others fall, we stand.

O Lord, grant salvation to your chosen; answer us when we call to you.

18

Psalm 20

The king, your anointed, is happy in your strength. Gladly he gives credit to you for victory.

You have granted him his heart's desire; you refused not the wish of his lips. He asked life of you, and you gave him length of days for ever and ever.

His kingship he received from you, and to you he passed on the triumph that his kingship brought him. The triumph, he knew, was yours and not his.

You gave him the happiness of your abiding presence, of your everlasting blessing. He trusts in you, and therefore stands as one secure.

Be praised, O Lord, in your strength. We will sing, we will chant the praise of your might.

†

Psalm 21

My God, my God, why have you forsaken me? Why do you stand afar off—too far to hear my prayer and the cry of my heart?

O my God, I cry out by day and you do not answer; by night and there is no relief for me.

I know you are there, on your throne in the sanctuary, but still you do not hear. You heard our fathers when they cried to you. They called and you answered them. They were not disappointed.

I am a worm and no man. I am dismayed when people say of me, 'He trusted in God; let God deliver him.' I am ashamed when they say, 'If God loves him so much, let God come and help him.'

All the same I do trust. You have been my guide and security from the first. Be close to me now, for I am troubled. Stay near, for there is nobody else to help me.

My courage is ebbing away. *My heart has become like wax melting. My throat is dried up like baked clay. My tongue sticks to my jaws. To the dust of death you have brought me down.*

A pack of evildoers closes in upon me. They have pierced my hands and my feet, they have numbered all my bones. They have stared at me. They have divided my clothes between them. They have cast lots even for what I wore.

But stay near me, Lord. Come quickly to help me. Rescue my soul in its loneliness.

I will tell of your glory to those about me. Publicly will I praise your name and say, 'Pay the Lord homage, all you who should be fearing God, and see what blessings he has heaped upon a wretched creature in his misery. The Lord has heard the misery of his servant and turned not away from him.'

So by your grace I will acknowledge you before all. Let those who are yet to be born have your message preached to them, that they in their turn may proclaim it to their generation.

All the ends of the earth shall remember and turn to the Lord. And to him my soul shall live. And those who come after me in my line shall be his servants.

☩

Psalm 22

The Lord rules me, and I shall want for nothing. He has turned my soul towards him, has set me in the midst of peace, has let my eyes rest on things of beauty.

And because he leads me along the right way, the darkness of the valley has no terrors for me. 'You are at my side,' I can say as I walk among the shadows.

Even to my earthly wellbeing the Lord is attentive. My cup brims over, my plate is stacked high.

Nothing but God's mercy follows me all the days of my life. I pray that I may go on living in God's house like this until the end of my days.

Psalm 23

Just as the earth belongs to God, so do the souls who dwell on it. And who among such souls will mount to where God himself dwells?

The soul who is without blame, who is clean of heart, who is shy of vanity, who is open with other souls: such a one shall be blessed indeed.

Of souls like this it can be truly said that they seek the face of God. It will be souls like this who give to the Lord the welcome he expects.

To them he will come as they open their gates to him. Who is this king of glory to whom they give welcome? *The Lord of hosts; he is the king of glory.*

☦

Psalm 24

I have lifted up my soul to you, Lord, and in you I have put my trust. Let not this hope be disappointed.

To look to you and then be left without support is not to be thought of. How one's enemies would gloat!

Make your ways known to me, Lord, and teach me to walk as you have planned that I should. *Guide me in your truth and teach me, for you are God my saviour, and for you I wait all the day.*

Remember how you have shown me pity before, and how I have relied on your mercies. Do not bring up my past sins, Lord, but think only of the pardon they look for.

Your goodness is my hope. If I can only keep your mercy before my eyes I shall come near to you in humility and trust. *For your name's sake you will pardon my guilt, O Lord, great as it is.*

To those who fear him, God opens up the way they should choose. *The friendship of the Lord is with those who fear him. My eyes are ever towards the Lord, for he will free my feet from the snare.*

Look in my direction, Lord, and have pity on me. I am lonely and hard pressed. Do something, please, about my worries.

Put a stop to my upsets I beseech you, and blot out also my sins. There are many against me, many who hate me; from these I ask to be delivered—as I ask to be delivered also from my sins.

I wait for you, Lord, so let my good intention be taken into account. Integrity and uprightness must surely amount to something, and anyway I look to you for my salvation.

✟

Psalm 25

I have trusted in you without wavering, Lord, and have done my best to be honest. Just try me and you will see.

I have made it my aim to act according to your truth. I have set your own charity before me as a model. I have not gone along with the godless and the fraudulent; in fact I have avoided them all I could.

I am more at home among the innocent, the religious, and the grateful. I enjoy being with you in your earthly habitations: the glory of your tabernacle delights me.

Please do not rank me among the men of violence, among the tough. I am doing my best to walk among the singleminded, among those who look to you for their salvation. I hope that I am settled on your side of the line. Have mercy on me accordingly.

✟

Psalm 26

The Lord is my light and my salvation; whom shall I fear?
The Lord is my life's refuge; of whom shall I be afraid? Though I am attacked on all sides, I shall not lose trust.

I do ask one thing of the Lord: that I may live in his house all the days of my life. That my eyes may gaze towards his beauty, that I may visit his temple continually.

22

For he will shelter me in his house when there is trouble, and establish me on the rock of safety.

Even as it is he has lifted me above my attackers. So I can offer sacrifices with shouts of gladness. Even as it is I enjoy the freedom of his tent. So I can sing the praises of the Lord with gratitude.

Hear, Lord, the voice which I raise to you. Have mercy on me and listen to my cry. My heart speaks of you, my eyes search for you, my whole self yearns for your presence.

Hide not your face from me; do not in anger repel your servant. Though my own parents reject me, yet will you take me up. Show me your way, Lord, and lead me.

I believe that even in this life I shall enjoy your blessing. The thing to do is always to wait for the Lord with courage. I must show spirit, and keep on waiting.

✠

Psalm 27

I shall call out to you, Lord, so be not deaf to my cry. If you pay no attention to me I shall only go downhill.

Hear the pleading words which go up to you, see the hands raised before your holy shrine.

Number me not among the unfaithful, the reprobate. They are following a different way.

Be praised, Lord, for you have heard the sound of my pleading. You give me strength, you give me shelter. In you I can trust for the help I need. To you do I lift up my song of gratitude.

Lord, refuge of your chosen one, bring salvation to your people. Rule them, bless them, and take their needs upon yourself for ever.

Psalm 28

Bring to the Lord, you followers of his, the glory and praise which are his right. Pay homage to his name in the temple but see him also in the works of his creation.

The voice of the Lord is over the waters. The God of glory thunders as his voice rolls over the sea. *The voice of the Lord is mighty, is majestic,* is able to split great trees—even the cedars of Lebanon.

The voice of the Lord is in the flash of lightening, in the earthquake, in the hurricane. The voice of the Lord is in the tornado which strips the forest bare.

Enthroned over the flood is the Lord, and from his throne he rules the earth. May he give grace to his people, may be bless them with peace.

✠

Psalm 29

I will pay homage to you, Lord, because you have snatched me away from danger. I cried out to you and you kept me close.

In answer to my prayer you have healed me. You have raised me from the depths. You have preserved me from contact with evil.

We, who by his grace are faithful, must show gratitude to the Lord. If sometimes he punishes us, always his mercy is there for the asking. We may go to bed humbled, but in the morning we can rejoice in his pardon.

One day, feeling very safe, I said to myself 'I shall never be upset again.' It was a day on which you had given me strength, Lord. But next day you hid your face, and I was terrified.

To you I cried out, Lord, pleading with these words: 'Why give me life at all, if in the end I go down to the depths condemned? Would my ashes be any thinks to you? Would I be witness any more to your grace?' *Hear, O Lord, and have pity on me. O Lord, be my helper.*

You changed my dejection into gladness. My sackcloth you took away and put on me the garment of joy instead. So now my soul can sing praises to you without end. O Lord, my God, I will give thanks to you for ever.

✠

Psalm 30

I have hoped in you, O Lord, and I shall never be disappointed. Turn your ear towards me, and hurry on my deliverance.

Be to me my protection, my stronghold. You are indeed my rock of safety; you will support me, lead me, free me from the chains that hold me fast.

Into your hands I commend my spirit. You will redeem me, O Lord, O faithful God. I will rejoice in your mercies. You have taken my humiliation into account, saving me and putting me on my feet again.

Have mercy on me, O Lord, for I am distressed; my whole life seems wasted. Sighing and sorrow have been my lot. My very bones are bent with the heaviness I suffer.

I am forgotten like the unremembered dead; I am like a dish that is broken. But my trust is still in you, Lord. I keep repeating, 'Your are my God . . . my affairs are in your hands.' In your great mercy, save me.

All these prayers cannot be lost on you. There must be so much goodness stored away—goodness which can be spent on those who fear your name.

Let those who take refuge in you be guarded by your presence; screen them in your temple from those who wish them harm.

I said once in my anguish 'I am entirely cut off . . . God has wiped me from his horizon.' Yet all the time you were listening to the cry I was putting up to you.

Listen, all you who remain faithful, and remain under God's loving care. Take courage, all you who hope in the Lord, and show spirit. Your hearts shall be kindled anew.

Psalm 31

Happy are those whose sins are blotted out. Happy is that man who stands without blame before God. To be without blame or guile is to be blessed indeed.

For as long as I shrank from admitting my guilt I wasted away in misery. Night and day the hand of the Lord stirred my conscience, and I wasted away.

Then at last I confessed my sin to you, disguising nothing. 'I acknowledge all my faults to the Lord,' I cried, and at once I received your pardon. Here is surely a grace which every man should pray for.

I shall be able to enjoy the freedom which by your grace is everywhere about me. The sorrows of the wicked are many, but the worst is their slavery to sin. Those who trust in the Lord are at peace in his blessings. They know liberty and can be glad with his joy.

☩

Psalm 32

Rejoice in the Lord, you religious people; praise is particularly your work. Give thanks on all kinds of musical instruments; sing a new song to him, and with shouts of joy proclaim his glory.

The Lord is worthy of all this and more. His works as well as his mercies deserve it. Creation demands homage to the Creator. God's plan overrides the plans of men; God's love for each single soul entitles him to our trust.

We must wait for the Lord who is our safety and our joy. May your love, O Lord, be with us who have placed our hope in you.

☩

Psalm 33

I will praise the Lord at all times. My lips shall not cease from the sounding of his praises. By rendering this tribute I shall encourage others, and they will rejoice.

Come, all of you, and join me in the work of praise. Look to him that you may share his joy and mine. Only taste this fare of praise, and you will know how good God is.

There will be nothing lacking to those who fear, trust, and praise him. The worldly are ever in danger of losing their possessions and going hungry; not so those who seek God and trust in him.

Listen, I will teach you true religion. Which of you wants to live fully and enjoy your time on earth? Well, the secret is to speak evil of none and avoid occasions of sin, to do good and follow the way of peace. Those who keep this rule receive God's blessings; those who act against it receive his punishments.

The Lord is close to the sad of heart. *Those who are crushed in spirit he saves. Many are the troubles of the just man, but out of them all the Lord delivers him.*

✠

Psalm 34

Take up my cause, Lord, and join me in fighting my battles. Remind me that you are yourself my victory.

My enemies try their tricks against me, but I know that so long as the Lord is on my side I have nothing to fear. Indeed I can maintain my soul in joy.

When others were overcome or ill, I brought them sympathy. When I myself suffer these things, the very people whom I compassionated turn against me.

For how long, Lord, must this go on? Seeing the unfairness of it, will you never take notice? Be not a passive witness to my humiliation, Lord, but counter the malice of my oppressors with your might.

Let those who say 'Aha, we were hoping for this . . . we have smothered him at last' be shown otherwise. And let those who work in my favour shout for joy and be glad.

Psalm 35

The man whose heart is already prone to evil is easily enough persuaded to sin. With him there is no fear of God to act as safeguard.

He deceives himself with false comfort. 'I shall not be found out' he says, 'and anyway God will not mind.' Such reasoning is empty; it only goes to show how far his understanding has been misled.

His conscience does not reproach him; he does not shrink from evil any more. His course is wide of the mark.

Lord, your mercy is without limit; you have a mind to save all living beings. How greatly we should value your goodness to us; how constantly we should shelter under your protection.

We are filled by all that is best of your treasures; we are refreshed by your waters. *For with you is the fountain of life; and in your light we shall see light.*

✝

Psalm 36

Do not be envious of evildoers; their prosperity withers like grass. For true security you must trust in God and do good. If you delight in the Lord you will find your petitions granted.

Entrust the direction of your life to God; he will see that it comes out right. Leave everything to him, and wait upon his word.

It is no good getting angry about the way in which the sinner always seems to thrive. You only upset yourself. Besides, the sinner does not thrive for ever.

Even the memory of the sinner is forgotten: the just, on the other hand, leave a mark. The Lord laughs at the sinner's show of wealth; the poor man's earnings, on the other hand, he respects.

Smoke evaporates, flowers wilt in the meadows. Do not yearn for the worldly possessions which last hardly much longer.

Speaking to you in my old age I can say that neither now nor in my youth can I point to the case of a just man being left stranded by God. *Though he fall, he does not lie prostrate, for the hand of the Lord sustains him.*

The just man is kind, is willing to lend. Instead of having to beg bread, his descendants shall be blessed. The law of God is in the just man's heart; he will not stagger in the way nor crumple up under trial.

I remember seeing a wicked man, and thinking how solid he looked: *stalwart as an age-old tree and flourishing.* Yet even as I passed by, his day was done. I looked for him but he was nowhere.

✝

Psalm 37

Lord, do not punish me in your anger. Your hand lies heavy upon me. Your arrow are deep in my flesh. My health has gone. And all this because of your indignation, because of my guilt.

I cannot endure the weight of my sin. My sores are festering because of my folly. I am bowed down with grief, aching in every limb, numbed and crushed and moaning in anguish.

O Lord, all my desire is before you; from you my groaning is not hid. I am drooping with weakness; even my sight fails me.

Friends and enemies alike avoid me. I do not hear what is said about me, and anyway I have not the voice to reply. You, O Lord my God, will answer for me. I rely upon you to take my part.

Always on the verge of falling, always conscious of my grief, always admitting my guilt. *Forsake me not, O Lord; my God, be not far from me. Make haste to help me, O Lord my salvation.*

Psalm 38

I said to myself, 'I must take care not to sin with my tongue; I must control my speech.' And although the evildoer stood before me I kept to my resolve.

If outwardly I was silent, inwardly I was in a turmoil of grief and anger.

Tell me, Lord, when to expect the end of my days. The span of my life is as nothing. All human existence is like a breath of air, a puff of smoke.

A man stores up a lot of possessions, but who is going to use them after he is gone? What am I waiting for, O Lord, if not for you alone? You are my hope. I am not living so as to leave a legacy; all earthly goods disolve like cobwebs.

I am but a pilgrim before you, a man walking along a road. It has been the same with my fathers before me. Keep sight of me all the same, Lord, if I am to find relief between now and the day of my death.

☩

Psalm 39

I have waited, waited expectantly for the Lord. He bowed down to me and heard my cry. He lifted me out of the swamp, and set my foot on firm ground. A song, too, he gave me to sing.

In your plans for us there is none to equal you. If I tried to make a list of the wonders you do for us I would find it beyond me.

You have not asked for sacrifice of mine: what you want is my obedience. Such holocausts as I might offer would be valueless without submission to your will. Better for me to say, 'I come to do your will, O God, and to observe your law which must always be the desire of my heart.' This is what has been decreed of me, and you see how I now come to fulfill it.

I have proclaimed your justice before all; your mercies I have not kept to myself. Men may say what they like, but my trust is still in you. Though reduced to poverty, I know that you are thinking of me all the time.

You are my helper and protector. O my God, do not delay your coming.

☦

Psalm 40

Blessed is the man who feels for the needy and the humble; the Lord will feel for him in the day of his own misfortune. The Lord will keep him safe and make him happy; the Lord will not let him be destroyed by his enemies.

The Lord will help him in sickness, will even cure him if it is to his soul's good. 'My enemies are just waiting for me to die' I once told the Lord, 'they are pleased that I am beyond recovery.' But you have not allowed their hopes to come to anything. And by this do I know that you love me.

You have looked at my sincere desire to please you and, seeing it, you have established me in your sight for ever. *Blessed be the Lord, the God of Israel, from all eternity. Amen. Amen.*

☦

Psalm 41

As the hind longs for the running waters, O God, so my soul longs for you. My soul is thirsting for God, the living God. When shall I be free to come before you? When shall I be able to stand in your sight and see you?

Waiting for this day, I have wept. And my longing has been all the harder to bear because of what others have said to me. 'Where is this God of yours whom you are always expecting?' they have asked.

Even when all are keeping high festival, celebrating with joy and thanksgiving, I am lonely in my vigil. Why are you so sad, O my soul, and why these deep sighs? Now is the time

31

to hope in the Lord. Now is the time to have confidence in your coming.

I keep on asking myself why I am sad. Always I know the answer. Always I know that I have no need to be sad, for you, O Lord, are all my hope.

Hope in God. For I shall again be thanking him, in the presence of my saviour and my God.

✝

Psalm 42

O God, judge my cause for me. Deliver me from the unbeliever, from the deceitful, from the faithless. Why do you keep me so long at arm's length?

Why must I always go about in mourning and melancholy? Send me your light. Your light will guide me to your holy mountain, will bring me at last to where you live. Send me your light and your truth.

Then will I go up to the altar of God, the God of my gladness and joy. It is he who gives joy to my youth. To him will I give thanks on the harp.

Why are you so downcast, O my soul, and why do you groan within me? You must hope in God, for soon again you will be thanking him in the presence of your saviour and your God.

✝

Psalm 43

Our ears have heard what our fathers have told us. We have learned what you did for your chosen ones long ago. How you ousted great nations to make room for your people.

By no power of theirs did our ancestors win the land they occupied. The conquests they made were by the strength which came from you. And so it has been ever since.

Yet today you have cast us off, and we march alone into battle. You have allowed us to be driven back by our enemies. We have been made fair game: we are open to plunder on all sides.

We are as sheep for the slaughter. We are sold off cheap at the market. We are scorned, laughed at, and ashamed.

Yet we have not betrayed you nor been disloyal. In all our distress we have remembered your mercies and counted on them.

Why do you sleep, Lord? Awake and stand up, and cast us not off for ever. Why do you hide your face, turning away from our misery?

Our very souls are bowed down to the dust, our bodies are ground into the mud. Rise up and help us. In your great mercy rescue us.

♰

Psalm 44

My heart overflowing, I chant the praises of my king. My tongue runs on as smoothly as a pen in the hand of a fluent writer. The tributes which I bring to my sovereign are these:

You are fairer than the sons of men. You speak words of grace. You are blessed by the Lord.

Gird your sword upon your thigh, most powerful one, and strike out with might in the cause of truth. Ride high, and show your might.

Your throne is established for ever. You love justice and hate iniquity, and therefore God has anointed you with the oil of gladness.

Your royal robes are fragrant with spices, your palaces echo to the sound of stringed music, the daughters of kings beg audience of you.

The fairest of the royal train of daughters is the Church, the daughter of the king himself. *Hear, O daughter, and see; turn your ear, forget your people and your father's house. So shall the king desire your beauty. For he is your lord, and you must worship him. All glorious is the king's daughter.*

Psalm 45

God is our refuge and our strength; he helps us in all our tribulations. So there is no reason to fear.

Though the whole world may shake and mountains fall headlong into the sea, though oceans rage and hills tremble, the Lord is with us still.

Though nations disintegrate and kingdoms stagger, though the earth itself disolve, the Lord is at the heart of everything and there is nothing to worry about.

God can impose his will upon the world which he has made. He has stopped wars before now, and for him it is not a difficult thing to break bows, shatter lances, burn shields.

'Forget your worldly way of thinking' he tells us, 'and see that I am God, mighty above all nations and mighty upon the earth.' The Lord of hosts is with us; he is our protector.

☩

Psalm 46

Clap your hands, all you nations, and shout to God with cries of gladness. For the Lord of the world has subdued our enemies; he has chosen us for himself.

Sing praise to him as he mounts his throne. For the king of the earth is God, and man must praise his name.

God reigns over the nations; God is enthroned in holiness. The princes of the nations are united with the people of our God. So sing praise to our king, sing praise.

Even those who rule the world and keep its peace belong to God. God is supreme above all.

Psalm 47

Great is the Lord, and worthy to be praised. Let him be praised in his city and on his mountain.

The kings of foreign lands stand in awe and wonder. They know they have nothing to boast about in the fact of such majesty.

Here is the capital city whose ruler' is God. From here God extends his sway; from here his justice orders the world in wisdom, charity, and peace.

We sing to our God for ever and ever; eternally he will guide us.

☦

Psalm 48

Listen to this, all you peoples who dwell in the world; whether of humble or high birth, whether rich or poor, pay attention to this prudent thing which I am telling you; there is wisdom in it.

In no way, I say, can a man redeem himself nor pay his own ransom to God. The price would be too high.

A man can see wise men die. He can also see foolish men die. Either way there is little enough left to posterity. So it shows the vanity of trusting to earthly things.

Death is the shepherd of those who flock after vanity. Like sheep they are herded down the slope into the next world.

But for myself I look forward to no such end. God will redeem me from the powers of evil, and will receive me among his own.

So when you see a man growing rich, remember that he takes none of his wealth with him to the grave. To him men may have said during his prosperity, 'Congratulations on having done so well for yourself,' but this will not help him if he dies condemned.

Man, for all his splendour, if he have not prudence, resembles the beasts that perish.

Psalm 49

God the Lord has spoken. He has summoned to himself the earth. He calls the heavens as witness. His beauty everywhere proclaims him.

'I want my servants, the faithful, to stand before me,' he says, 'those who have made a covenant with me in their sacrifice.

'I, the Lord, am speaking to you. It is not your sacrifices that offend me. Indeed, though I need not the victims you offer,' your holocausts please me always. So go on with your work of sacrificing.

'What offends me is the lack of true spirit behind these sacrifices. What offends me is that these sacrifices are not backed up by obedience, justice, honesty and charity.

'Neither covenant nor sacrifice counts for anything when those who make them fail to live up to the terms laid down.

'Do you think that I, with whom these covenants are made and to whom these sacrifices are offered, have not noticed the fraudulence in all this? Do you think I am like yourselves, satisfied with the ceremony and quick to forget the meaning of the ceremony?

'When your life matches your sacrifices you render me true praise, and I will reward you. But be careful that your ceremonial is not a screen for malice.'

Psalm 50

Be merciful to me, Lord, according to your great goodness. Wash away utterly my sin.

I admit my guilt. Indeed it stares me in the face the whole time. I was born sinful, tarnished from my mother's womb, and I know that to acknowledge it sincerely is pleasing to you.

You cleanse me and you teach me wisdom at the same time. I pray that you may make for me a new heart and place in me a right and steadfast spirit.

Do not throw me over, and let me not be deprived of your holy spirit. Renew in me the joy of salvation, and confirm in me the attitude of willingness.

I undertake to correct the wayward, teaching them your way and urging them to return to it. Lord, open my lips so that I may pronounce your praise.

If you call for sacrifice I will offer it. Better than the holocausts which displease you is the offering of a humble and penitent heart. This I know you will not reject.

☩

Psalm 51

Why do you delight in evil, you who have become expert in infamy? You never stop planning harm. Razor-edged, your tongue cuts deep with malice.

You choose evil rather than good, lying rather than truth. You love all that spells destruction. Honesty is not in you.

God will break you up for good. He will pull you from your tent, uproot you from the land of living men. The just will look on and wonder.

And then the just will laugh and say, 'This is the man who thought he could do without God . . . who trusted in wealth and cunning.'

But all the while I shall be trusting in God, flourishing like the olive tree in his presence. I will give thanks always for what the Lord has done, proclaiming his goodness before all the faithful.

☩

Psalm 52

'There is no God' said the fool in his heart. This is typical of people who do evil. And certainly there is hardly anyone who does good.

Looking down from heaven upon mankind, God has to peer closely to discover even a single soul who is wise and who seeks him. *All alike have gone astray; they have become perverse; there is not one who does good.*

Are these evildoers never going to learn? When will they start calling upon God? They are tormented by fear, but they fear all the wrong things.

When God restores his people, then will men talk sense and be happy.

✞

Psalm 53

Save me for your name's sake, Lord, and by your power defend my cause. Hear my prayer, O God, and listen to the words of my mouth.

You are my helper; you support my life. Gladly will I offer you sacrifice. I will praise your name, Lord, for its great goodness.

You have plucked me out of all my distress. My eye can now look down upon my enemies.

✞

Psalm 54

Listen to my prayer, Lord, and do not despise my pleading. Hear me and answer me. I am troubled. I sway about with grief. I fear persecution.

My heart flutters with fear inside me; the dread of death overshadows me. Trembling has come upon me and horror overwhelms me.

'If I only had the wings of a dove' I sigh to myself, 'I would escape and be at peace. I would fly afar off, and hide myself in solitude. There I would shelter from storm and turmoil.'

If an enemy had reviled me I could have borne it. But when my friend, the one with whom I stood side by side in the worship of God, turns against me I am brought low indeed.

But I will call upon God, and the Lord will save me. He will give me peace from those who war against me. Smooth is their speech and oily, but war is in their heart. Their words are so many drawn swords.

Cast all your care on God, and he will support you; never will he permit the just to be destroyed. Men of blood and treachery shall not live out half their days. For my part, I trust in you, O God.

☩

Psalm 55

Have pity on me, O God, for men grind me under their heels all the day long. I am always being trampled on.

When fear seizes me I remember your promises, and this gives me hope. What, after all can human beings do against me?

Though they may plan every sort of evil against me, they still have you to reckon with. So long as I have confidence in you I can snap my fingers at opposition.

My dedication to you is unshaken. I will pay your thank-offerings to the full. You have delivered me. You have prevented my feet from stumbling. All this you have done that I might walk before you in the light of the living.

☩

Psalm 56

Take pity on me, O God, for in you I place my trust. I shelter under your wings till the threat passes by.

O God, most high, I look to you as my benefactor and saviour. I pray you send help from heaven and deliver me.

Though many are ranged against me, I hold steadfast'y to you. I do not mean to change: I will sing your praises for ever.

I stir up my soul to watchfulness and song. At the dawn you will hear my hymn of thankgiving. I will proclaim it in front of everyone.

Be exalted above the heavens, O God, above all the earth be your glory.

✠

Psalm 57

I am addressing myself to you, you men of position. How do you stand in regard to justice? How ungodly you are who pretend to godliness, to fairness, to honesty.

Your gains are ill-gotten, your steps are turned away from truth, your speech is poisoned. You are snakes, and as snakes can be deaf to the charmer's flute so you have made yourselves deaf to the calls of grace.

Be careful or you will find your teeth smashed in your mouths. You will be like water draining away; you will be like the wax which melts and vanishes. Like the thorn-bush in a whirlwind you shall find yourselves swept off the face of the earth.

There is one reward for the just, another for the wicked. *And men shall say*: '*Truly there is a God who is judge of life.*'

✠

Psalm 58

Defend me from those, O God, who bear a grudge against me. Save me from the malice of evildoers, from those who are out for blood.

Stir yourself to see my need, Lord, and break down this opposition to me. My enemies think there is none to listen to my prayer, but you can laugh at them and uphold me.

Come to my assistance, O God, and defeat the plots which are daily hatched against me.

And I will sing of your strength, and revel at dawn in your mercy. You have been my refuge in the day of distress.

☩

Psalm 59

Lord, you have rejected us. Why is your anger turned against us? Our walls are down, and there is none to help but you.

Our people are divided, and the whole country is tottering. Come quickly to repair the cracks and heal the wounds.

You have allowed hardships to come upon us, and we feel burdened beyond endurance. Save at least a remnant, and we shall be grateful.

Are you failing us at this stage, Lord, that you go not with us into battle? Let us enjoy your help again, Lord, for there is no help to be gained from men.

Under God we shall do valiantly; it is he will will tread down our foes.

☩

Psalm 60

Hear, O God, my prayer; listen to me while I pray to you. From the ends of the earth I cry to you; and my heart grows faint with calling.

May you give me rest, my refuge. It is you to whom I look as to a rock, as to a tower.

I only wish I could lodge in your tent for ever, and under the protection of your wings.

You have received my vows; you have granted me the heritage of those who serve you in fear. *So will I sing the praises of your name for ever, fulfilling my vows day by day.*

41

Psalm 61

Is not my soul at God's disposal? From him alone comes my salvation. Nothing will uproot me any more, so long as I make him my whole security.

Will they always so pounce upon a man as to beat him flat? Will they level him with the ground as though he were a sagging fence, a crumbling wall?

I make God my stronghold, my rock of support. At all times, my friends, we must trust in him. So pour out your hearts to him, and trust.

Mortal men are no more reliable than a breath of air. Those in high office are transparent, insubstantial, an illusion. Weigh them, and put all together they turn out lighter than a puff of air.

Though wealth abound, set not your heart upon it.

Here is one very important truth which you must know. It has a twofold message: all power belongs to God, and with that power goes mercy.

☩

Psalm 62

O God, my God, I have been up early waiting for you. My soul thirsts for you; with my whole being I long for you. In a hundred ways I stretch myself out to you.

Parched, lifeless without water, the earth craves for rain. So do I crave for you. I gaze in your direction to see your power and glory. Your mercy is a greater good than life. My lips glorify you.

So shall I praise you while I live. Lifting up my hands I will call upon your name. And my soul shall be satisfied as a man is satisfied by the lavish fare of a banquet.

If I wake during the night I will remember you; before the dawn I will contemplate you. For you are my helper, and your wings are spread to protect me.

Let all who invoke you find glory, and let the mouths of those who deny you be utterly stopped.

☦

Psalm 63

Listen, O God, to the voice of my lament. Too many there are who bear a grudge against me and are pledged to do me harm.

But you can shoot arrows at them and bring them down. Whatever their boast of cunning and independence, they cannot stand against you.

Let all men fear and proclaim the work of God; let them ponder upon the meaning of his acts. *The just man is glad in the Lord, and takes refuge in him; in him glory all the upright of heart.*

☦

Psalm 64

Our vows must be paid to you, O God, for the answer that you give to our prayers.

To you all living beings must come, O God, for the debt that is owed by sin.

That man is happy whom you choose, O God, for the place which he fills in your courts.

If I set myself to tell of your glory, O God, there will be no end. The mountains you have put in their appointed place; the waves of the sea you regulate.

The earth you make rich by sending down rain upon it, and from its drenching you raise up its harvest. The fields are clothed with flocks, and the soil of the valleys is covered over, as by a blanket, with corn.

43

Psalm 65

Rejoice, all you on earth, and proclaim the glory of God's name. Tell the Lord how magnificent are his works, and how all mankind is come to praise his name.

Come and see the works of God, his tremendous deeds among men. For our ancestors he has changed the sea into dry land, so that through the water they might pass on foot.

Certainly our faith has been tested, O Lord. *You have tried us as silver is tried by the fire.* You allowed us to fall into a trap; you put burdens on our backs. You let horsemen trample us down.

Yes, we went through fire and water, but you have led us out of all this. So I will offer sacrifice in thanksgiving; I will pay you my vows. My holocausts to you shall be worthwhile tributes.

Hear now, all you who fear God, while I tell you what he has done for me. He has heard me; he has listened to my prayer. Ah, blessed be God who has not denied my petition nor withheld his mercy.

☨

Psalm 66

May God take pity on us and bless us. May his face be light and grace to us who look towards him.

So may we see what way to take upon this earth. So in the midst of this world may we walk towards salvation.

May all mankind praise the Lord. May all peoples be glad that you rule in justice; may they know that it is you who guides them.

The earth has brought forth to harvest, for the Lord our God has blessed us. May he continue to bless us, and may we acknowledge him in holy fear.

Psalm 67

The Lord has risen and his enemies are scattered. His enemies have evaporated like smoke; as wax before the fire so have they melted away.

But the just are firmly set; they rejoice before the Lord and regale him with song.

They sing of him as the father of orphans, the defender of widows, the protector of the homeless, the deliverer of captives.

O God, what a shower of mercy you have rained down upon your people. You have restored your weary people, providing for them at every turn.

Blessed day by day be the Lord who bears our burdens; blessed be God who is our salvation. The Lord our God arranges for our salvation; the tunnel through death he prepares. He takes our part in the struggles of life.

Awesome in his sanctuary is God, the God of Israel. He gives power to his people. Blessed be God.

☩

Psalm 68

Save me, O God, for the waves are breaking against my soul. I am sinking into quicksand, and there is no foundation under my feet. I am down as far as I can go, and the flood washes over me.

I am exhausted with calling out for help, and my throat is sore. My eyes grow dim with looking for my God.

Not one of my faults is hidden from you, yet must I restore what I did not steal? I have become an outcast to my own family, and all this because zeal for your house is burning me up.

I humbled myself with fasting, and it only made people resentful. I put on sackcloth, and people laughed at me. Though gossips babbled, and drunkards made jokes about me, I have not stopped praying to you, O God.

So let not the flood-waters altogether drown me, let not the swamp suck me down. But answer me in your great mercy. Deliver me from my foes.

I looked for sympathy and there was none; for comforters and I found none. Rather they put gall in my food, and in my thirst they gave me vinegar to drink.

The Lord hears the poor, and his own who are in bonds he spurns not. The descendants of his servants shall inherit the land, and those who love his name shall inhabit it.

✛

Psalm 69

O God, decide to rescue me; O Lord, be quick and help me. Let those be turned back who advance against me; let them go home in disgrace.

But may all who are looking for you be glad. Let them go on always saying 'Glory be to God.'

But as for me I am upset and in poverty. O God, be quick to help me.

You are my helper and deliverer. O Lord, do not delay.

✛

Psalm 70

I have put my hope in you, Lord, so let me not be disappointed. In fairness listen to me and deliver me. You are the firmament of my life, my only refuge.

What patience I have, Lord, is yours that I share with you. You are the grounds of my hope, and always have been. From my infancy I have been settled in this confidence.

Do not abandon me in my old age. *O God, be not far from me; my God, make haste to help me.*

Though I cannot know how long I shall live I do know that I shall continue to praise your name to the end. You have taught me from my youth, and I am still making known your wonderful works.

So now that I am old and gray, Lord, do not leave me alone. Though you have allowed me to feel the weight of trials, Lord, I know that there is none like you. You will revive my spirit. You will raise me from the dust.

Renew your mercies to me, Lord, and console me again and again. So will I give you thanks. At least I shall not forget your mercies; at least I shall be found giving praise to the end.

My tongue day by day shall discourse on your justice.

Because I am unlettered and ignorant I must depend upon God alone. It is his wisdom, not mine, which must carry me through.

You have taught me from my youth, Lord, and to this very day I have proclaimed your great works. So do not let me down in my old age.

I have seen trouble in my life, and always you have pulled me through. From out of the depths you have raised me, comforting me with your closeness.

No wonder I have cause to confess your truth and goodness. If my lips were never to cease in your praises, I would still not have said enough.

Psalm 71

Let him who rules be guided by your wisdom, Lord, and let judgment be given fairly. Let the ruler be merciful to the poor, and let the tyrant be made helpless.

Let the saviour who is to come be received with thanksgiving. Like the rain falling softly upon fleece, like showers soaking gently, so may he take his place in our midst.

In his days shall justice spring up and the world shall know peace. *He shall rule from sea to sea; and from the river unto the ends of the earth. All the kings of the earth shall adore him; all the nations shall serve him.*

For he shall deliver the poor from the mighty, and the needy that has no helper. He shall save the souls of the poor . . . and their names shall be honourable in his sight.

Blessed be his name for ever. The whole world shall be filled with his greatness, shall ring with his majesty, shall resound to the glory of his name.

☦

Psalm 72

God is certainly good to his chosen people, to those whose hearts are towards him. But my own heart has not always been towards him: I saw what seemed to be the good fortune of the wicked, and I lost confidence in the Lord.

But the lot of the wicked, however prosperous outwardly, is not to be envied. Their iniquity will finally bring them down.

They may say 'How can God know about us and our sin?' They may ask what God sees of their acts. And at first sight they seem to have wisdom on their side: sinners *do* manage to escape the wrath of God.

It was exactly this which made me think I had been good to no purpose, that I had been a fool to resist the lure of the world. Why, I asked myself, had I wasted so much time in doing penance?

But then I turned to prayer for the answer, and the answer came to me in the sanctuary of the Lord. Having worked it all out in God's presence I knew beyond doubt the conclusion of the matter.

The sinner does not go scot free. Just when he imagines himself safe in his sin, then is he marked down for destruction. His image of security has no reality: it is the stuff of dreams; it is a fancy.

I see now what a beast I have been, how my doubts have degraded me. I am not worthy to be called a man. Yet all along you have supported me. You have been close beside me, holding my hand and guiding me like a father guides his son.

And now *what have I in heaven? And apart from you what do I desire on earth?* Those who stray away from you are doomed to perish, but when a man clings close to you he must survive. It is good for me to cling close to my God, to put my hope in the Lord. So shall I sing the praises of the Lord; publicly I will profess him.

☦

Psalm 73

Why do you abandon souls like this, Lord? How can your anger be roused against those whom you call your own? We are sheep of your pasture; we are members of your flock.

You have kept us from the beginning. Are you confusing us with your avowed enemies? Ah yes, your enemies have plotted against you. They have made it their whole task to uproot religion from the land.

And up to a point you have let them have their way. But as for us we have always held to you as our God. You have been our king from the start.

We have seen the works of creation, and have attributed them to your power. We have seen nations overturned, and have traced your hand in the working of it.

But now, Lord, deliver not up to beasts the souls that confess you; and forget not at the last the souls of your poor. Remember the pact which you made with us. We are the obscure ones; let us not be turned away. It is the poor and the needy who give you the greatest praise.

Psalm 74

We will praise you, Lord, and will call upon your name. We will recount the tale of your wonders; we will issue warnings to the wicked.

God, our God, is judge over all. One he overturns, another he raises up. In his hand is held a cup of strong wine. He pours it here, he pours it there. But always there are dregs left over. And of these dregs the sinners of the world must drink.

But I will declare the glory of the Lord for ever. With the strength that he gives me I will overthrow his enemies.

☩

Psalm 75

God is known in his own country, in the Church which he has established. His place is there more than anywhere else; his place is in peace.

Lord, you give light most wonderfully from your everlasting hills. And when you are angry there is none to stand against you. When you pass judgment the world stands still to listen.

The very thought of man is so much praise to you. Therefore let man pay his vows to God; it is in such promises, faithfully kept, that the mind of man makes holiday.

All you who stand round about the Lord, bring presents. The Lord can be terrible when he wants to be. He can break to bits the great ones of this world. So pay your debts to the Lord, and offer to him the gift of sacrifice.

Psalm 76

With my voice I cried out loud to the Lord. I cried to him and he heard me. In the day of my trouble I looked for the Lord. All night long I stood before him with my arms stretched out. Nor was I disappointed.

After a time when my soul rejected comfort I remembered the Lord. I turned to him, and my soul was flooded with joy. I was faint with sheer delight.

And again I was troubled, keeping vigil the night through and never talking. I went back upon the past, probing my soul and fearing expulsion from God's sight.

But will he cast me off for ever? Will he not take me back again? Are his mercies dried up? Has his anger overridden his will to forgive?

Then came a day when I knew I had begun afresh. 'I am starting again' I said, 'and it is the right hand of God that is bringing this about.' I remembered how the Lord had acted before, and I knew that this was none of my doing.

From now on I will think only of your works, Lord, and set myself wholly to your service. Your way, O God, is holy. There is none like you. Your way is seen in the direction of the world. You have led your chosen ones like sheep.

✝

Psalm 77

Listen to the words of my law, all you who follow me, and pay attention to what I say. *I will open my mouth in parables.*

Now all these things have been handed down to us. We have no excuse for not knowing what the Lord has said. From generation to generation his message has been passed on.

But many have forgotten this covenant of the Lord's, and it will be to their shame and regret. They should consider, these faithless ones, the miracles which rescued their ancestors. Have they turned their backs on what happened to their fathers?

51

Well, it has been like that all along. Even while God showed his miraculous protection, even while wonders were multiplied for them, there were those who hardened their hearts.

So now too: his mercy is there for the asking, but souls abound who will have none of it. *Man ate the bread of angels.* But all the while men went on sinning. *They believed not his wondrous works. Their days were consumed in vanity and their years in haste.*

Only when he began killing them did they turn to God. Then they came back to him, appealing to him in the early morning. Then they remembered who their helper was, and how the most high God had saved them.

But even now they loved him only with their lips; their hearts were untrue. How could this be counted as fidelity to the covenant? But here is the wonder of it—that despite all this he will be merciful. He will forgive and will not destroy.

Again and again he turns away his anger. Ready to acknowledge that his creatures are creatures indeed, as likely to return thanks as a breeze which blows across the desert and does not bend back on its course, the Lord makes allowance for weak flesh.

Time and time again he leads his people like sheep. He takes dangers away from their path, he defeats their enemies, he feeds and clothes and shelters them. But they still go on tempting him, doubting him, failing him in their covenant.

Even when he punishes them, and he does so only to draw them closer to himself, he does not go all the way. Lest he break their spirit, he spares them before the time.

And now at the last he has given them a king.

Psalm 78

Unbelievers have taken over what is yours, Lord, and have defiled your sanctuary. They have reduced the holy city to a fruit-market, they have allowed the bodies of your faithful to become carrion.

Your servants have spilled their blood all about Jerusalem, only to lie unburied and as meat for beasts of prey.

Among neighbouring peoples our name is mocked. We are laughed at in our defeat. If your anger has been turned against us, may it not now be turned against those who oppress us?

Forget our guilt, Lord, and let not our record of sin stand against us. Poor and discouraged, we are at the end of our tether. Has the hour not come for the display of your mercy? For your own greater glory deliver us, O Lord. For your name's sake, Lord, deliver us.

Judge what will happen if we go down before our enemies and yours. Will not the unbelievers ask, 'Where is their God?' They know that we are the sheep of your pasture. Do this thing for us, Lord, and we will give thanks to you for ever. From generation to generation we will proclaim the glory of your name.

✝

Psalm 79

O ruler of the tributes of Israel, listen. Stir up your power, Lord, and come to save us. Convert us, Lord, and we shall be saved. Show us your face and all will be well.

O Lord God of hosts, will you turn away the prayer of your servant for ever? Are tears to be my lot right up till the end?

You have made us to be your own special vineyard. You furnished your vineyard with all that was best. Do you now let it run to waste? The hedges are broken and poachers come in at will. Your precious vineyard is at the mercy of animals.

Turn again, O God of hosts, and look down from heaven. Come to visit this vineyard of yours. Cultivate once more that which your right hand has planted, and bring to perfection that which once held such promise.

Let your blessing be upon the man whom you have chosen, upon the son whose inheritance you have confirmed.

We will not leave you, Lord, because in you we have life. Convert us, O God, and we shall be saved. Only show us your face, Lord, and we shall be saved.

☦

Psalm 80

Let us delight in God our helper; let us sing aloud to the Lord. Now a song, now a musical instrument, now a feast. These are things which give praise to the Lord.

'You called out to me in your trouble' he says, 'and I delivered you.' Yes indeed he has heard us. But have we heard him? 'My people heard not my voice,' he complains, 'so of course I let them go according to the desires of their heart . . . if they want to walk in their own ways they must learn their lesson.'

Had we only listened to his voice we would have been sheltered by the Lord from all our enemies. It is always the same story: lies and treachery on the part of man, mercy and sweetness on the part of God.

He fed them with the fat of wheat; and filled them with honey out of the rock.

☦

Psalm 81

Strange gods may be honoured by others, but for us we have the one true God. He stands in the midst of them and passes judgment upon them.

54

He passes judgment also upon the lesser powers, upon the rulers and leaders and judges. He reproaches them for their injustice and for the way they tread upon the poor.

'It is the poor whom you should be helping,' cries the Lord, 'it is the needy whom you should be rescuing from the hands of the sinner.'

Unjust rulers forego their claim to divine authority. Mortals and not gods, they die like everyone else.

Arise, O God, and judge the earth; for you shall inherit among all the nations.

☦

Psalm 82

Who can be compared to you, O God? Speak out, Lord, and do not rest. Your enemies have made a great stir: they have conspired against you and against your people.

But their power is neither in noise nor in cunning: you can silence them with a word, you can turn their plans inside out.

Let them plot as much as they like, but their plotting will go up in smoke. Your flames shall run after them and consume them utterly. Their faces shall be darkened with shame.

All must know that the Lord is God. *You alone are the most high over all the earth.*

☦

Psalm 83

How lovely are your tabernacles, O Lord of hosts. My soul longs and faints for the courts of the Lord. My heart and my flesh have rejoiced in the living God.

As the sparrow finds its shelter, so does my soul find its rest in your house and among your altars. Blessed are they that find lodging with you, Lord, for they will praise you for ever.

Blessed is the man who has you for his helper. He will mount up from the valley of tears to the high slopes which you have prepared for him.

O Lord God of hosts, hear my prayer; listen, Lord, while I cry to you. One single day spent with you is better than thousands spent anywhere else. I would rather be wretched in your house than merry in the houses of sinners.

You will not allow the innocent to go without. Blessed is that man who trusts in your goodness.

✝

Psalm 84

You have blessed your land, Lord, and have brought back your people from captivity. You have forgiven your children their sins; you have covered up the evidence of their malice.

You have softened your anger; you have cancelled your intention to punish. Convert us instead, Lord, and bring us a new life. Show us mercy and we shall be saved.

I must listen to what the Lord has to say to me. To his own he speaks peace. To them that are right of heart he brings salvation.

Mercy and truth have come together in union. Justice and peace are one. Truth is sprung up from the earth; justice has looked down from the heavens. From the Lord comes all this goodness.

✝

Psalm 85

Turn your ear towards me, Lord, and hear me. I am poor and in need. Look after my soul because I strive after perfection. Save me because I trust in you.

I have cried to you all day, Lord, so have mercy on me. Let this soul of mine which I have lifted up to you, O God, know joy. Joy and sweetness are yours to give, and there is a generous mercy waiting for those who beg for it.

Attend to my prayer, Lord, and let not this petition go unheeded. In the day of trouble I have called to you. You have heard me before in my distress.

So it is also with the nations: you have raised them to stand before you and adore. They shall glorify your name and you will be merciful to them. You alone are God.

Lead me along your own way, Lord, and I shall walk according to truth. I will praise you because my heart shall rejoice. Your mercy has been the ground of my hope. You are the God of compassion, patience, truth.

Psalm 86

Let your holy Church be praised: the Church which is founded upon a mountain, upon rock.

Great things are said of you, O city of God. By the highest himself you have been established.

In his scriptures the Lord speaks of you. Your noble names, the names of your elect and of the saints, are recorded.

The dwelling in you is as it were of all rejoicing.

Psalm 87

O Lord, the God of my salvation, night and day I have raised my voice to you. Now let my prayer come in before you. Only listen to my petition.

My whole soul is flooded with wrong; I feel myself being sucked down into hell. I am numbered among the damned.

Like a dead man in his grave, forgotten and cast off. I am sunk to the lowest depths. All is dark in this shadow of death.

Your anger has towered over me. Waves of it have broken upon me. Even my friends you have estranged from me. They despise me, and I am alone.

I have invoked you but apparently to no purpose. Is it because I am dead that you waste no more graces on me? Are you saying, 'What is the good of showering mercies on men already buried?'

But I cry to you still, and in the morning my prayer shall be there waiting for you. Do not be deaf to this prayer, Lord, and do not turn away your face from me.

I am poor, and sorrow has been my lot since I was young. Exalted at one time, but humbled and troubled too.

✝

Psalm 88

The mercies of the Lord I will proclaim for ever. His truth I will declare for all generations to hear.

The Lord has made clear his policy regarding us. He has told his chosen people that they can rely on his mercy. 'I have established them' he has said, 'for ever.'

O Lord, your truth will be evident in the Church. There is no power like yours, and mankind must acknowledge this. Truth and the strength to bear witness to the truth: these are qualities which may not be denied.

As creator you are lord of all. As protector you reveal your mercies. As judge you expound your truth.

Men shall walk in the light of your face. In your name they shall rejoice. On the strength of your justice they shall be exalted.

Then you revealed the mystery of the Incarnation. 'I have brought help to one that is mighty,' you said, '*and exalted one chosen out of my people.* I have found David my servant, and with my holy oil I have anointed him. No enemy shall have power over him. Satan is in chains against him.

'*My truth and my mercy shall be with him, and in my name shall his horn be exalted.* And if David's sons shall fail me I will punish them but not cut them off. My covenant stands. Truth shall be in my Church for ever. Truth and mercy: these shall belong together in my Church for all time.

I have sworn it, and my word shall not be made void. Remember this, you who doubt and defy the revelation of God. Do not forget the nature of your God; recall what my very substance is; my essence, my being, is known to you. Just as it is your nature to fall and trust and fall again, so it is my nature to speak truth and show mercy.

So I have not made men in vain. I have remembered, for my part, what their substance is. Men cannot live for ever; nor have they power over one another for eternity. But for my part I have eternal life, and can bestow eternal life one way or the other.'

Lord, be faithful to these words of yours. Remember what you swore to David. May you be blessed, Lord, for ever. So be it. So be it.

☩

Psalm 89

Lord, even before the mountains were fashioned from the earth which was your creation, you have been God. And at the coming of man you have been his refuge.

Your summons stands: you call us to repentance.

Time is not the same with you as with us. A thousand years are as yesterday to you. Man's day is like the grass: it springs up, lives for a while, and when evening comes is dry and withered.

In the light of your face the sins of man stand out to reproach him. Whatever his span of years, man has nothing of his own in which to place his trust. A spider's life, that is all.

Aye, Lord, you have a right to be angry. Man has not a leg to stand on. Yet can he still take heart and cry for mercy.

Return, Lord, in mercy. Despite our wretchedness we rejoice. We take our delight in you. We delight in the memory of humiliation. It was good for us that we saw hard times.

Keep on directing our ways, Lord, for we are your children and your servants. May your light be upon us always, directing our lives and the work of our hands.

✠

Psalm 90

The man who lives under the Lord's protection will be able to use for his song words like these:

You are my refuge, O God, and I trust in you. You have delivered me from snares, from stinging words; you allow me to shelter under your wing. Your truth shall be a shield to me. My soul is no longer afraid of the night-time terror.

The arrow, the ghost, the demon: be they there in daylight or in darkness to menace us, they cause fear no more.

Know this, you who enjoy the Lord's protection, that a thousand may fall at your side—or even ten thousand at your own right hand—but you shall be safe.

It is hope in the Lord that counts. So make the most high your refuge. He has given angels to look after you; their hands will support you.

Though you walk among deadly animals you will still be safe. No harm can come to you at all.

'Because he hoped in me,' the Lord has said, 'I will deliver him. I mean to protect him because he has known the power of my name.

'He shall cry to me and I shall hear him. I am with him in his distress; I will deliver him and I will glorify him when his day comes.

'I will satisfy his longing with everlasting life. I will show him salvation which is mine alone to grant.'

✠

Psalm 91

It is good to give glory to God, to sing the praises of his name. It is good to declare his mercy in the morning and his truth at night.

How pleasant to sing your glory to the accompaniment of musical instruments. O Lord, you have given me pleasure in praising your name, and I delight too in the works of your hands.

Your works are vast and your thoughts are deep, but none of this is known to the fool. The stupid man cannot understand the meaning of things.

The wicked spring up everywhere like grass, and like grass they shall perish. But you are eternal.

Because I have been faithful I can trust in your mercy. You will not fail me in my old age. A just man shall flourish like a palm tree. He will remain rooted and erect like a cedar. Such are those who are planted in the courts of God. God himself will see to it that they bear fruit, and that in old age they will not be wanting.

✠

Psalm 92

The Lord has reigned, and is clothed in beauty. He wears his strength like a garment. He stands girded for battle and strong.

Nor shall the world be moved which he has established. Lord, your throne is made ready. It always has been made ready because you are God from all eternity.

Like waters in full flood, with waves roaring their message, your wonders may not be gainsaid. Your truths cannot be denied. Your holiness will be manifest for ever.

✝

Psalm 93

Where revenge is needed, the Lord has it to show. He can be free in meeting out retribution. Iniquity is not to go unnoticed.

They that kill the widow and the stranger will have an account to render. The man who murders the fatherless is in for judgment.

No good saying that God will turn a blind eye. He who gives sight must surely see. He who has fashioned the ear must surely hear.

The Lord knows how foolish are the thoughts of men. Blessed is that man whom the Lord teaches and who learns the law of the Lord. Unless the Lord had taught me thus, I certainly would have sunk to the depths.

I had only to admit my weakness and the Lord came to my rescue. According to the multitude of my miseries were the consolations which flooded my soul.

So the Lord is my refuge. He is the ground of my hope.

Psalm 94

Come with me and praise the Lord with joy. In gladness of heart let us sing to God our saviour.

Let us come before him in thanksgiving; let us please him with song. For the Lord is God, great and powerful. He is king over all, creator and master of mankind.

Come let us lie down before him and adore. Let us weep for our sins in his presence. For he is our God and we are his people.

So *today if you shall hear his voice, harden not your hearts.* Our ancestors hardened their hearts and offended him. He swore he would punish them and he did.

✟

Psalm 95

Sing a new canticle to the Lord. Let all the world sing to him. With each new day let his praises be sung. Let the unbelievers come to know his wonders.

For the Lord is great and exceedingly to be praised. He is also to be feared.

Homage and beauty stand before him always; holiness and majesty are with him in his Church. All men, believers and strangers to the truth alike, must bring glory to the Lord.

Let us for our part offer sacrifices in his sanctuaries; let us adore the Lord in his holy courts.

Let all the earth be moved in his presence, and may mankind at large acknowledge his rule. He is, after all, the judge of every man, and if nature proclaims his majesty so also must the human race.

The Lord will rule the world with justice. He will bring truth to his people.

Psalm 96

The Lord has ruled so let the world rejoice. Though mystery veils the sight of him, he reigns from a throne of justice.

Flame precedes him, scorching his enemies round about, and his lightnings bear witness to his wrath.

Mountains can perish before him like melting wax, so overwhelming is his presence. The heavens bear witness to his justice, so let those beware who worship idols.

Lord, you are mighty; you are exalted over all. Your followers see this and rejoice. All bow before your judgments.

All you who love the Lord steer clear of evil. The Lord looks after his servants, delivering them from the power of evildoers.

Light is risen to the just, and joy to the right of heart. Be glad in the Lord, you who are faithful, and delight in calling to mind his holiness.

✝

Psalm 97

Sing to the Lord a new canticle, for he has done wonderful things among us. He has stretched out his right hand to save; his arm is strong in holiness.

The Lord has revealed his sanctity; his justice he has made known before all. Nor has he withheld his mercy, and to the whole Church he has proclaimed his truth.

All the ends of the earth have seen the salvation of our God. So let all the world sing gladly to God, praising him on the harp and with trumpets.

Let all natural creation join in praise. The sea, the mountains, the rivers: let these works of his hands be witness to his presence.

The Lord comes to judge the earth; he will judge the world justly. His people will know fairness at his hands.

Psalm 98

The Lord has reigned and has angered his people. But it is for them to give praise to the Lord and to fear him. He may be frightening but he is also holy. By his very nature he must have justice.

You men of God's creation should exalt him above every other power. Remember those who have been numbered among his followers, among his faithful servants. Moses and Aaron among his priests, Samuel ever calling upon his name.

Yes, they called upon his name these servants of his, and he heard them. And when they did what he told them, obeying his laws, he listened to their prayers. He showed himself full of mercy towards them.

So let us pay homage to the Lord our God. *For the Lord our God is holy.*

Psalm 99

Raise a cry of joy to the Lord, all you who inhabit the earth, and see that you serve him in gladness.

Come before him with delight in your hearts. His presence invites you to happiness.

You must understand that this Lord of ours is God himself. He made us; we did not make ourselves. We are his people, the sheep of his pasture.

Come, cross his threshold with praises upon your lips. His courts must resound with the canticles of his servants.

Let us together give glory to his name. The Lord is loving. His mercy and truth endure for all time, and generation after generation shall taste of their benefits.

Psalm 100

I will sing to you, Lord, of mercy and judgment. And then, when you come to me, I shall understand and see the way clear, the way to perfection.

I have trodden the path of innocence. Occasions of sin I have avoided. Evil companions are not for me. Indeed the wicked avoid me.

The man I have been hard upon is the one who speaks evil of his neighbour. I have entirely rejected him. Nor will I sit down to eat with the proud and the rapacious.

Instead I like to have the faithful near me, the kind who seek perfection. Let such people wait upon me, not those others.

Proud men shall enjoy no hospitality from me; the unjust shall not benefit from what belongs to me.

☩

Psalm 101

Hear my prayer, Lord, and let my cry reach you. Do not turn your face from me. Especially when I am in trouble, Lord, listen.

But in whatever day I call upon you, Lord, be swift in answering. For my time is running out. Like smoke I am drifting away. Like sticks for the fire my bones grow brittle with age.

My heart is like the fading grass. I neglect my food, and my flesh is withering. I lie awake at nights and am more like a bird—a raven, a pelican, or a lonely sparrow on the housetop —than a man.

The only fixed thing in my life is my faith in you. You are permanent, you endure for ever. Your mercy can be counted upon, and those who pray to you shall have safety.

We must know that the Lord hears the groans of those enchained, that he frees from slavery the children of the slain. They will declare his graces.

All visible creation shall pass away but you, the creator, shall remain. Men shall grow old and die: one gives place to another as one garment is exchanged for another. But with you there is no change: you go on the same for ever.

✠

Psalm 102

O my soul, bless the Lord. Let all that is in me praise his holy name. Never let me forget what he has done for me. He has pardoned me my sins and healed my afflictions.

He has redeemed me from destruction, shown compassion in my distress, satisfied my longing with good things. He has renewed my youth.

The Lord does not deal with us according to our guilt. But high as are the heavens above the earth, so is his mercy above what we deserve. As far as the east is from the west, so far has he taken away from us our shame.

As a father has compassion on his children, so the Lord has compassion on those who fear him. He knows us. He sees that we are dust. He remembers that we are but grass.

To those who keep his law the Lord makes good his promises. So bless the Lord, all you angels. You servants of his who do his will, praise his name. And you, O my soul, pay homage to the Lord in every place and in all his works.

✠

Psalm 103

Bless, O my soul, the Lord God who is exceeding great. O God, you are clothed in praise and beauty. You are wrapped with light as with a cloak.

You have stretched out the sky like the roof of a tent. You have set the clouds racing like chariots. You ride the winds.

You make foundations on which the earth must rest. Oceans wash its surface, covering even the mountains. At the voice of your thunder there is fear, there is flight.

By your command the desert flattens out and the hills rise up. There are bounds set by your wisdom to the expanse of water. The waters shall not come back to flood the earth any more.

You summon springs to rise up in the valleys, and between the hills the rivers are made to flow. Beasts can drink, and in the rocks the birds can nest.

From the yearly rains come forth the harvest, and man and beast are fed by its yield. Thus bread comes out of the ground, and wine to cheer the human heart. Oil too for the well-being of man.

Leaves come to garland the trees, and here the sparrows make their homes.

You arrange the seasons, Lord, ordering the course of the sun and moon; night and day take their obedience from you. Man goes out to his work in the morning and comes home again in the evening; the hours of his day are spaced out by you.

Creatures small and great lean ever upon your wisdom. All look to you for the food which sustains them from season to season. How great are your works, Lord. How wisely you have planned your world, filling it with good things.

The moment you look away, everything goes wrong. The breath of life is stilled, and flesh returns to dust. *Send forth your spirit and they shall be created; and you will renew the face of the earth.*

I will sing to the Lord as long as I live; I will sing praise to my God while yet I have my being.

Psalm 104

Give glory to God and call upon his name. Make known his acts to those outside the Church. Tell of his works with praise and song.

Let those who seek the Lord rejoice in heart. Seek always the Lord and be strengthened in your search. Never stop looking for his face.

Remember the wonderful things he has done; remember the wisdom of his judgments. He is the Lord our God, and it is because of his grace that the world goes round.

He makes covenants with man, and abides by them. He protects his own people, and will not allow others to harm them. When famine reduces the land, he supplies what is needed for life.

Remember what happened when Joseph was chosen to rescue God's people from starvation. And then there was Moses who again provided enough, and more than enough, for the support of life. Signs and favours were multiplied in those days.

All this was because God remained true to his word, the word which he had spoken to his servant Abraham. Accordingly he led out his people with joy, his chosen ones with lightness of heart.

He gave them the lands of unbelievers to dwell in . . . *that they might observe his justifications, and seek after his law.*

✠

Psalm 105

Give glory to the Lord for he is good. His mercy can be counted on for ever. Who shall do justice to his wonders?

Blessed are they who are faithful to him, who live up to his graces at all times. Remember us, O Lord, in your loving-kindness; grant us the salvation which we seek.

We are eager to see the evidence of your working, Lord, and especially in the happiness of those who serve you.

By our sins we have forfeited our claims upon your favour, but because of our surviving faith we still have hope. Again and again we have failed you as a race—our whole history is a list of infidelities—but we always crawl back to ask your pardon.

And when you see us in our tribulation you hear our prayer. You remember your covenant, and your mercies flow out to us once more.

And he gave them unto mercies in the sight of all those who made them captives. Save us once again, O Lord, and gather us in from our scattering among foreign peoples, *that we may give thanks to your holy name, and may glory in your praise.*

Blessed be the Lord, the God of Israel from everlasting to everlasting. And let all the people say, 'So be it, so be it.'

☦

Psalm 106

Give glory to the Lord for he is good; his mercy endures for all time. May those who have been redeemed by him acknowledge his goodness—those especially who have been brought back from among strangers.

What loneliness and privation they suffered, these exiles, and now he has delivered them from all their distress. He has led them into the right way at last.

The mercies of the Lord are witness to his glory; his works stand as proofs to the minds of men. *He has satisfied the empty soul, and has filled the hungry soul with good things.*

Many there were who withered away in darkness, awaiting death in privation and chains, and this through their own fault. To provoke the Lord is to ask for trouble, and these men had provoked the Lord and were paying the penalty.

Weakened, humbled, helpless, they cried to the Lord. He rescued them from their distresses. He brought them out from the shadow of death, breaking their fetters and refusing to hold against them their guilt.

He turned the storm into a breeze, and its waves were still. Let the record of his mercies give glory to the Lord. Let his followers exalt him in the Church, praise him in his throne. The just shall see and shall rejoice . . . *who is wise and shall preserve these things* . . . who is true and will understand their meaning?

✝

Psalm 107

My heart is ready, Lord, my heart is ready. I am only waiting to sing of your glory. In the morning early I will praise you.

Among all the people and before all the nations I will confess you. Your mercy to me has been infinite, and of your truth there can be no end. So I must proclaim your wonders with all my might.

If I am looking for salvation, who but you can give it to me? If I want to be led in the right way, who but you can be my leader?

Will you not march with our armies, Lord, and protect us in battle? *Vain is the help of man. Through God we shall do mightily, and he will bring our enemies to nothing.*

✝

Psalm 108

Be not silent, Lord, in taking my part. Everyone else is speaking against me, spreading falsehood and taking away my good name.

I showed love, but my love was wasted on them; so I gave myself to prayer. When people put on evil like a cloak, it is hard to have dealings with them.

71

But because of your mercies I look to you in my loneliness. I beg to be delivered for I am poor and in need; my heart also is troubled within me.

I am declining like a shadow. People shake me off as they would shake off locusts from a tree. People look at me and wag their heads. *Help me, O Lord God; save me according to your mercy.*

Only save me and I will give thanks; before all I will praise you. You are there at the elbow of the poor, to save people like me from their persecutors.

✝

Psalm 109

The Lord said to my Lord, 'Sit at my right hand until I make your enemies your footstool.'

The Father will give to his Son the sceptre, the sign of his power. He will tell his Son to rule in his name.

With the Son is all authority. From him comes the light of the saints. Before the first morning star shone in the heavens, the Son was begotten of the Father.

The Lord has given his word, and he will not go back on it: *You are a priest according to the order of Melchisedech.* He has said this thing, and he will support it if need be by shattering with his anger the rival claims to kingship.

God himself shall judge among nations. He has power to crush those who lift up their heads against his power.

✝

Psalm 110

I will praise you, O Lord, with all my heart. Where the just are gathered together I will proclaim your glory.

Great indeed are your works, carried out according to your design. Everlasting is your justice; nor shall the homage to your majesty ever cease.

In your mercy you have fed those who fear you. You will not forget what you have promised. You will make clear your designs to your people.

Your commandments are just, confirmed eternally and framed in truth and equity.

You have granted salvation to your people; you have established your covenant for ever. Holy is your name, and worthy of awe. *The fear of the Lord is the beginning of wisdom.*

☦

Psalm 111

Blessed is the man who fears God: he shall find peace in God's commandments. His descendants moreover shall receive God's support.

In his house shall be glory and abundance; the fruit of his judgment shall be lasting.

To the upright of heart is risen up a light in the darkness. The Lord is merciful, compassionate, just.

Now the man who imitates the Lord in mercy, who lends his goods with generosity and gives consideration to his words, shall be pleasing to God. Not for him to be moved, not for him to be forgotten of the Lord.

Hope is his strong suit, and openhandedness his expression. He will not go unrewarded. The wicked shall take note of this and be envious. And well may they be envious for the desire of the wicked shall perish. Too late then to grit their teeth and show anger at the blessedness of the upright.

Psalm 112

All of you, give praise to the Lord. Sing loud to his name. Yes, now and until the end of time.

From sunrise to sunset the Lord is to be glorified. He stands high above the nations which he has made; high even above the heavens.

Who is like the Lord our God who rules over all? From his dwelling in the heights he looks down upon his creation.

Those in need he raises up, the poor from their wretched surroundings, and places them among the great ones of his people. To the homeless and the childless he gives shelter.

☩

Psalm 113

When the chosen people of the Lord came out of captivity there was joy as well as trembling in the world round about.

Nature was turned upside down before the face of the Lord. The sea retreated in full flight, the mountains leapt, and fountains of water sprang up where there had been none before.

So there was no excuse for unbelievers to question the existence of our God. Our God is in his heaven still; he has done all that he wanted to do.

The gods of the heathen tell a very different story. Made of silver and gold by the art of man, they have nothing to say for themselves. With mouths that are dumb, ears that are deaf, hands that touch not and feet that walk not, the gods of the heathen are small comfort to men.

Let those who fashion such images come themselves to resemble them. Let the followers of the Lord, on the other hand, come more and more to trust in God. Our hope is in him who helps and protects.

The Lord has remembered us and blessed us; he blesses all who fear him and trust him.

The heaven of heaven is the Lord's, but the earth he has given to the children of men. We who live must bless the name of the Lord, now and for ever.

☩

Psalm 114

Because the Lord will hear the voice of my prayer, therefore I have come to know the meaning of love. In all my days on earth I will call upon him, and he will hear me.

If the sorrows of death are overwhelming me, at least I am still clinging to my prayer. The Lord is merciful and just: therein lies my hope.

The Lord watches over the little, the humble, and the poor. I am of no account, yet before now he has delivered me.

Rest, O my soul, in this knowledge. Never have you been let down when you trusted. Be determined to please the Lord while you have life in you; time out of number he has come to your rescue.

☩

Psalm 115

I have believed; therefore I have spoken. But I have been humbled exceedingly.

'Every man is a liar' I said, exaggerating.

What return shall I make to the Lord for all that he has given to me? I will grasp the chalice of salvation, of suffering, and will call upon God's name.

I will fulfil my vows to the Lord. Publicly I will pronounce them, and publicly keep them. Precious in God's sight is the service of those who die to self.

Such a service I mean to render, Lord, for I am your servant as my mother was before me. You have made me free to serve and to sacrifice.

I will render to you the sacrifice of praise. I will call upon your name and be faithful to my vows. In the sight of all your people, in the courts of your house, in the heart of your holy city, I will serve you in sacrifice.

✝

Psalm 116

Let the whole world praise the Lord: everyone, everyone.

For his mind is set in mercy, and his truth remains for ever.

✝

Psalm 117

Give praise to the Lord for he is good; for his mercy endures for ever.

Let all his people admit now that he is good, and that his mercy endures for ever. Let those that fear him repeat it. I myself, when I am in trouble, must repeat it.

The Lord is my helper; I do not fear what man may do to me. It is good to have this confidence in God: better than to put trust in man. It is idle to trust princes.

My enemies swarmed round me like bees, but in the name of the Lord I was saved. They struck me to make me fall, and once again the Lord supported me.

So the song of rejoicing and thanksgiving is heard among the faithful. From the tents of his followers goes up the cry: 'God's right hand is mighty: it has raised me up.'

I shall live and not die; I shall live to declare the works of the Lord. I shall be able to show evidence of his mercies.

Open to me the gates of justice, and I will pass through them to praise the name of God. These are the Lord's gates and the just shall enter in by them.

I will pay homage to you, Lord, because you have heard me and are my salvation. *The stone which the builders rejected; the same has become the head of the corner. This is the Lord's doing and it is wonderful in our eyes.*

This is the day of the Lord; we must rejoice in it. *Blessed is he that comes in the name of the Lord.* You are my God and I will pay homage to you.

Praise the Lord for he is good; for his mercy endures for ever.

✠

Psalm 118

Blessed are they who keep the commandments of the Lord, who study his word, who seek him with all their hearts.

If only I can live up to this. Help me, Lord, and I shall learn the secret of your perfect service.

How does a young man control himself? Surely by keeping your precepts. And with my whole heart I have tried to do this, seeking you in the pages of your revelation.

Your words I have treasured, knowing that they would prevent me from committing sin. I must meditate upon your law, and forget nothing of it.

Open my eyes, Lord, to the beauty of your words. Give me grace to see and apply. I am but a pilgrim on this earth, and have need to know the way of truth.

My soul was weighed down, hugging the ground, but you have raised me up and given me cause to persevere. My soul slept, but you have woken me up. I have chosen the way of truth.

I have pledged myself to your law. No sooner did you enlarge my heart than I attached myself to your service for ever. I am committed.

Only give me understanding, and I will discover the inwardness of your law.

Turn away my eyes that they may not see vanity. Direct me wholly towards your commandments.

Reveal your word to me, Lord, and fix it in my heart. How I have longed to be set in the way of grace.

If people criticise me, let your word of truth be in my mouth. I must trust in your word of truth. It is your word that makes me free, that prevents me from feeling ashamed.

I have pondered your law and have come to love it. I have obeyed your commands and have come to love them.

Your word has given me hope. It has comforted me in my humiliation and has stirred me up. Remembering your decrees, the judgments you pronounced long ago, I was comforted.

Though I collapsed at the sight of so much wickedness all round me, at the neglect of your law in the world, I revived when I remembered your mercy. I remember your name in the night, and how I had kept your commandments, and I was no longer troubled.

I am ready and not distressed any more. Even if I am surrounded by wickedness, I need never forget the other side of the story. It is this that makes me get up at midnight to praise you.

The earth, O Lord, is full of your mercy: teach me your justifications. Teach me goodness and discipline and knowledge. Before you humbled me I offended you; but now that I am humbled I have learned to keep your word.

In your goodness teach me the good that lies in your law. *It is good for me that you have humbled me, that I may learn your justifications.* These justifications mean more to me than gold and silver.

I am a creature of your making: grant me the wisdom to read your law aright. Let my fellow creatures see in me the hope which you have planted.

Your judgments are fair. You were right to humble me. Only let your mercy be my consolation. You have pledged yourself to me your servant; only let your mercies be forthcoming and I shall live.

My soul has swooned in its longing for salvation, and in every word of yours I have trusted utterly. I have forgotten nothing of your justifications, of your testimonies. These justifications and testimonies are your word.

Your word is truth, and I am clinging to that. It may go by the name of statutes or commandments or law, but it amounts to your pledge. And you have pledged yourself to mercy.

For ever, O Lord, your word stands firm in heaven. It is proclaimed to all generations.

If this had not been the subject of my meditation, of my prayer, I would long ago have gone down. Instead the thought of your word has given me life.

So now I am yours entirely, yours because I have sought you in your commands. I am yours because I have loved what you have commanded. Through your commandments you have made me wiser than my enemies. Through them I have understood more than those who have taught me.

And now how delightful are your words to me. Yes, sweeter than honey. They are a lamp to my feet, a light on my path. If men have laid a trap for me they will be disappointed.

Receive me according to your word and I shall live; let me not be deprived of that for which I long. *Help me and I shall be saved; and I will meditate always on your justifications.*

I have followed you in judgment and justice, so do not hand me over to those who slander me. I have yearned for salvation, so deal with me according to your mercy.

Even to repeat your words gives light: it brings understanding to children. Your words are rare and purified, and though I am young and of no standing in the world I love them and do not forget them.

Before the sun rises I am already studying your words. They make me hope. I am able to say, 'You are present, Lord, and all your ways are truth.'

I have known about your words from the beginning, and *that you have founded them for ever . . . the beginning of your words is truth: all the judgments of your justice are for ever.*

I will rejoice at your words as a man will rejoice at discovering a buried treasure.

Seven times a day I have repeated my praise to you. For I know that to them who know your law and praise it there comes great peace. To them there are no doubts or stumbling blocks.

So let my petitions rise up before you, my hymns of praise and my appeals for mercy. My soul shall live and shall glorify you. And for your part your judgments shall help me.

I have gone astray like a sheep that is lost; seek your servant, because I have not forgotten your commandments.

✝

Psalm 119

I called to the Lord in my trouble, and he heard me. Lord, spare me from the evil which people say about me.

What good shall they get from their malicious tongues? So far as I am concerned they have had their way. I have lived long enough among these people, and am dismayed that my time is prolonged.

I showed them peace, but peace was not what they wanted. I spoke words of friendship to them, but was rejected.

✝

Psalm 120

I have raised my eyes to the mountains, because help will come to me from there.

My help is from the Lord who made heaven and earth. Unsleeping, he watches over his people.

The Lord will be your protection if you ask it of him. Ask this and you will be sheltered against every evil. Neither at night nor by day will you be troubled.

May the Lord guard your soul. May the Lord see to your coming in and your going out. May he do so now and for ever.

☩

Psalm 121

I was made glad by what was told me: 'We shall go into the house of the Lord.'

Our feet stood in the holy city's courts, in the city which is so exactly planned.

The people of the Lord go up to this city, paying homage to the Lord their God.

You must pray for the peace of this holy city. Pray also that good things may come to those who love you.

I too pray in this way, asking benefits for my friends and neighbours.

I have begged that peace may be yours, together with all other good things. For in the house of the Lord we share our benefits. Our strength is in this unity and peace.

☩

Psalm 122

I have lifted up my eyes, Lord, to you who are in heaven. Just as the eyes of servants are constantly watching the hands of their masters, so am I constantly looking at you until you give me the signal of mercy.

Have mercy on us, O Lord, have mercy on us. Contempt has been heaped upon us and has become part of us.

We have had our fill, and it is as much as we can bear. *We are a reproach to the rich,* and matter of contempt to the proud.

Psalm 123

If you had not been with us, Lord, we would have been wiped out. We would have been swallowed up alive.

We could not have withstood men's anger; we would have gone down before it. As it is we have passed through a torrent, all but submerged by the rush of water.

Blessed be God who has spared us, who has fished us out of danger. As a sparrow is released from the trap, so our soul has been released from captivity. The trap is broken and we are free.

Our help is in the name of the Lord, who made heaven and earth.

✠

Psalm 124

They that trust in the Lord shall be as safe as mount Sion. Their foundations shall not be moved.

Just as the holy city has mountains all round, so God's people have the Lord encircling and protecting them.

Sinners shall not have power over the just. The Lord will see to it that the just will remain just and not be corrupted.

Lord, give grace to the upright of heart, and whatever happens to the wicked let your followers be ever in peace.

✠

Psalm 125

When the Lord brought us out of captivity he filled us with consolation. Our mouths spoke gladness and our tongues were busy with songs of joy.

The unbelievers can say at the last: 'Their God has done great things for them.' And this is true indeed, for certainly he has. Yes, we have inherited joy.

They that sow in tears shall reap in joy. When your people went away they were weeping. But they were also sowing the seeds of future happiness. They have come back glad, bearing the fruits of their harvest.

Psalm 126

Unless the Lord build the house, they labour in vain that build it. Unless the Lord keep the city, he watches in vain that keeps it.

If you are sad, what is the point of getting up before the dawn? It only makes a sad day longer. Sleep is a gift from God. Children are a gift from God.

What weapons are to the mighty, children are to those whom sorrow has shaken. Blessed are those whose desire for a family of children has been fulfilled. A household of young people will be a man's support when he goes out to meet his difficulties in the world.

Psalm 127

Blessed are they that fear the Lord, that walk in his ways.

What the work of your hands has produced you shall eat with satisfaction; you have every right to such pleasure, for the Lord blesses it.

Your wife is like a fruitful vine, and your children are like the fruitful olive tree. This is the kind of blessing that comes to the man who fears God.

May the Lord bless you, and may you see these good things all the days of your life. May you see grandchildren in your family and peace among God's people.

Psalm 128

Your people can tell of how often the enemies of God have fought against them. 'From my youth' a follower of yours can say, 'I have had enemies on my back . . . but they have not brought me down.'

The Lord who is fair to his servants will see that the sinful do not triumph over the good.

The wicked will be like moss that withers on the roof, like grass that is tossed aside by the mower.

Passers-by have given no blessing. They are indifferent to blessings. But it is still for us to bless in the name of the Lord.

✝

Psalm 129

Out of the depths I have cried to you, O Lord. Lord, hear my voice. Let your ears be attentive to the voice of my supplication.

If you are to take account of all our sins, which of us can be saved? But mercifully we can expect pardon. Your law itself gives me reason to hope.

My soul relies on your word. My soul hopes in you. From sunrise to sunset let your servants wait upon you in hope.

Because with the Lord there is mercy, and with him plentiful redemption. And he shall redeem his people from all their iniquities.

✝

Psalm 130

My heart is not puffed up, Lord, nor are my eyes scornful. I have not presumed to handle things of importance, nor dabbled in what was beyond me.

How foolish I would be to pride myself about anything. Humility is far more suitable to my state.

Let me be as a child towards its mother, dependent for everything. Let all your followers hope in you. Not only now but for ever.

☩

Psalm 131

Lord, remember your servant, David, and the humility which was his. He made vows to you, and what he set himself to do was this:

'I must find out a place for the Lord, a tabernacle suitable for him to dwell in.' Such was his intention, and he would not rest until the need was met.

He wanted a place on earth for the Lord, a place where the ark might rest. He wanted to establish a priesthood, and it was his prayer that holiness should flourish in the land.

Now for your servant David's sake, Lord, turn not your face away. You made a convenant with David, promising great graces to his line. *If your children will keep my covenant,'* you told him, *'their children also for evermore shall sit upon your throne.'*

You said that since David had chosen the holy city as your resting-place, you would dwell in it. 'Here will I stay,' you said, 'for I have made up my mind about my house.'

☩

Psalm 132

How good and pleasant it is for brethren to live together in singleness of heart.

Such charity flows and anoints, and can be sensed by other people. It is like a precious ointment which runs down from the head to the heels.

It is like the dew which gently moistens the mountain's surface, the surface of the holy mountain.

It is here that the Lord orders all in blessing . . . blessing and life everlasting.

Psalm 133

All you servants of the Lord, now is the time to bless his name. You who stand in the Lord's house, in the very courts of God, lift up your hands in prayer.

At night-time and in the holy places, praise the Lord with arms uplifted.

May the Lord bless you from his holy city: the Lord who made heaven and earth.

Psalm 134

The name of the Lord be praised. All you, his servants, praise the Lord.

You who stand in the Lord's house, in the sacred courts, give praise to God.

Sing to the Lord for he is good; sing to his name for it is all delight.

Great and powerful is our God, and he has done whatever he pleased—whether in heaven or on earth, whether in the sea or in the sky.

Signs and wonders too he is master of. Consult our history and you will have proof of this.

So different from the heathen's deities. Idols have mouths which never speak, eyes which never see, ears which cannot hear. Let the makers of these images come to resemble those things which their hands have wrought.

For us let us bless the Lord. Let the houses and tribes of the Lord be constant in praising him.

Psalm 135

Praise the Lord for he is good, for his mercy endures for ever.
He is God, he is Lord, he alone does great wonders. His mercy
endures for ever.

In his wisdom was the world created, by his power were his
people saved, for his glory was his Church established. His
mercy endures for ever.

He has given us an inheritance, he has remembered our afflictions, he has saved us from our enemies. His mercy endures
for ever.

He has heard our prayer, he has given food to every living
creature, he takes care of all that he has made. His mercy endures for ever.

Give glory to the God of heaven, give glory to the Lord of
hosts. His mercy endures for ever.

☩

Psalm 136

We sat down weeping by the side of Babylon's rivers. We
remembered the holy city and were sad.

We hung up our harps on the branches of willows. We had
no heart for playing. Our captors asked us to sing to them the
songs of our own land.

But how can we sing, in this alien world, the hymns of the
Lord? It is not that we forget the Lord, or Jerusalem, or the
songs of our people.

*Let my tongue cleave to my jaws if I do not remember you,
if I make not Jerusalem the beginning of my joy.*

Remember us, Lord, and restore us to the holy place where
we belong.

Psalm 137

I will praise you, O Lord, with my whole heart. For you have heard the words which my lips have spoken in prayer.

I will sing to you in the sight of the angels. I will worship facing towards your holy temple, and will give glory to your name.

I will give thanks for your mercy and for your truth. You have made your name greater than all other names.

In what day soever I shall call upon you, hear me.

Be you praised by the mighty and obscure alike. All must know that you listen to our prayers.

If I find myself in the very thick of tribulation, I know you will be with me to give me spirit. So often your right hand has saved me.

Your mercy endures for ever, Lord, and because of this I believe that no creature of yours is beneath your notice.

Psalm 138

You have tested me, Lord, and you know what kind of person I am. All along you have known what I have been up to.

My thoughts you have known before they have come into my head. You have foreseen my way and predicted my speech. There is nothing about me which has been hidden from you.

This knowledge of yours is wonderful to me. Its effects are all about me, and yet I can neither pin it down nor hide from it.

If I wanted to fly from your spirit, where would I go? If I tried to avoid your face, how would I set about it?

If I were to mount into the skies you would be there; if I were to go down into the depths I would find you present. If I flew to the ends of the ocean, your hand would be already there to hold me.

At one time I said to myself, 'Perhaps darkness will cover me.' But I had forgotten that darkness is not dark to you: to you the night is as light as the day.

The truth of it is you possess me utterly, and are near me the whole time. *My bone is not hidden from you which you have made in secret . . . your eyes did see my imperfect being; and in your book all shall be written.*

Put me to the proof, O God, and see deep into my heart. Search my soul, and direct my ways. Look and see if I am following the wrong course. Only lead me towards everlasting life.

Psalm 139

Deliver me, O Lord, from the unjust and the sinner. There is poison in their talk, and they have tried to bring me down.

But I have cried to you: 'You are my God; listen to the prayer which I put up to you.'

I know that the Lord will do justice to the needy and will revenge the poor.

So those who are upright must give glory to the Lord. They shall live in the radiance of his face.

Psalm 140

Lord, hear me for I have cried to you. Let my prayer rise up as incense in your sight. Let the raising of my hands reflect the evening sacrifice.

Guard my lips, Lord, so that I neither speak evil nor make excuses for my sins. I am ready to be corrected by the upright, but I want no business with the sinner.

I have raised up my eyes to you, O Lord, and in you I have put my trust. Only keep me from the stumbling-blocks which the sinful leave lying about for me.

Psalm 141

I have raised my voice to the Lord, and before him I have poured out my prayer. When my spirit failed me, I told him my trouble.

I looked about for help and there was nobody to take my part. Flight was out of the question. So I called out to you.

'You are my hope,' I said, 'listen to my plea because I am brought very low. Lead out my soul from this prison so that I may praise your name. The souls of the just are waiting for me in heaven until the day when you reward me.'

☩

Psalm 142

O Lord, hear my prayer. Listen to my sincere petition. In the name of your justice hear me.

In your sight no living man is justified, so do not exact the full debt that is owed to you.

I am troubled, I am in anguish. I keep looking back over the past, and my spirit trembles at what I see.

I stretch out my hands to you. My soul is parched earth. Hear me soon, O Lord, for my spirit fails me.

Do not turn away from me or I shall stumble down and down. Let me in the morning learn of your mercy.

Make known your way to me so that I may walk along it. Teach me to do your will, for you are my God.

Your holy spirit shall lead me into the land where I am meant to dwell. You will bring my soul out of trouble . . . for I am your servant, O Lord.

Psalm 143

Blessed be the Lord my God who teaches my hands to fight and my fingers to war. My mercy and my refuge, my support and my deliverer.

He protects me and I have hoped in him; he keeps my people in order for me.

Lord, how has man deserved to know you? How is it that you notice us? Man is nothing but vanity; his life is a shadow.

When I think of the greatness of your creation I wonder at your concern for man. Put out your hand, Lord, and deliver me . . . for certainly you take heed of your creatures.

I will sing a new canticle to you, with psalms and harps, because you give salvation to kings, and because you have spared your servant David from the sword.

People who live in prosperity may be thought to have peace, but the truly happy are those who have the Lord for their God.

☩

Psalm 144

I will praise your name for ever, Lord; yes, for ever and ever. Every day I will do this, because you are greatly to be praised.

All future generations must do this too, declaring your greatness, and recounting your mercies.

Let the saints proclaim your glory, and let the work of your hands bear witness to what they claim. The saints must publish your truth.

Your holiness must be recognized—how you lift up the fallen, feed the hungry, keep your promises, and bless every living creature. All your dealings with man are just, all your works are holy.

The Lord is close to those who call upon him, to all who call upon him in truth. He will answer the prayers of those who fear him and will protect those who love him.

My mouth shall speak the praise of the Lord. Let all flesh bless his holy name for ever . . . yes, for ever and ever.

☦

Psalm 145

O my soul, give praise to God. As long as I live I will keep praising him.

To trust in anyone but God is madness. I have no confidence in the might of men. Men cannot save our souls for us.

Blessed is he who has God for his helper, who trusts in God alone. God is true; he keeps his word; he judges justly. God frees those who are in chains; he gives light to the blind and the souls who walk in darkness; he feeds the hungry.

Those who are dragged down, God raises to their feet again. He cares for strangers, looks after the fatherless and the widow. But he is stern when it comes to the sinner.

May the Lord reign for ever, from generation to generation.

☦

Psalm 146

It is good to praise the Lord. Joyful praise is suitable, and it pleases him.

Praise him for building up his holy city. He will gather into it the scattered from among his people. He heals the sorrows of the broken-hearted, he binds up the wounds of the afflicted.

Great is the Lord, and great is his power over all creation. Every star he knows by name. Has he not numbered them? There is no measuring his wisdom.

The Lord lifts up the humble, and brings low the wicked and arrogant.

Sing praise, then, to our God upon the harp. It is he who masses the clouds in the sky, who gets ready the rain which is to moisten the earth.

It is he who causes the plants to grow, plants which are for the use of men. It is he who sees that animals are fed, beasts and birds alike.

In return he takes pleasure in souls who fear him, in souls who hope in his mercy.

☩

Psalm 147

Praise the Lord, O city of the Lord; praise your God, O holy city. *He has strengthened the bolts of your gates; he has blessed your children within you.*

He has given you peace along all your frontiers, and has filled you with rich harvests.

He sends his speech to the earth; his word runs swiftly. He makes snow, looking like wool, to fall in due season. He distributes mists where they are needed. He commands winds to blow and waters to flow: all judgment in these matters is in his hands.

But to us especially are his favours granted; he has not done as much for every nation. Alleluia.

☩

Psalm 148

Praise the Lord from the heavens; praise him from on high. All you hosts of angels, praise the Lord.

Sun and moon, praise the Lord. So also stars and light. Heaven of heavens, praise the Lord, and let the waters that are above you do the same.

*Fire, hail, snow, ice, stormy winds . . . mountains and hills,
fruitful trees and cedars; beasts and all cattle, serpents and
feathered fowl, kings of the earth and all people; princes and
judges of the earth; young men and maidens . . . let the old
with the younger praise the name of the Lord. For his name
alone is exalted.*

Therein lies a hymn. It is sung to the glory of God's people.
It is apt for those who approach him. Alleluia.

✝

Psalm 149

Sing a new canticle to the Lord. Let the sound of his praise
be in the Church. Let his people rejoice in God.

From the choir let his name be praised. The Lord is pleasant
with his people; he will reward them. His holy ones shall rejoice for ever.

Songs of praise shall be in the mouths of his saints. *This glory
is to all his saints.*

✝

Psalm 150

*Praise the Lord in his holy places; praise him in the firmament
of his power.*

Praise him for his mighty works and deeds; praise him according to the greatness of his majesty. There is none so great
as he.

Praise him with the sound of the trumpet, with the psaltery
and with the harp.

Praise him in choir. Praise him with every kind of music and
instrument.

Praise him on cymbals, and especially with the cymbal of joy.
Let every soul praise the Lord. Alleluia.